THE *Feasts* and FESTIVALS OF THE *Messiah*

THE *Feasts* and FESTIVALS OF THE *Messiah*

LYNDA CHERRY

CFI

AN IMPRINT OF CEDAR FORT, INC.
SPRINGVILLE, UTAH

ISBN 13: 978-1-4621-4355-9

Published by CFI, an imprint of Cedar Fort, Inc.
2373 W. 700 S., Springville, UT 84663
Distributed by Cedar Fort, Inc., www.cedarfort.com

LIBRARY OF CONGRESS CATALOGING-IN-PUBLICATION DATA TO COME

Cover design by Courtney Proby
Cover design © 2022 Cedar Fort, Inc.

Printed in the United States of America

10 9 8 7 6 5 4 3 2 1

Printed on acid-free paper

Dedication and Acknowledgments

———— ❦ ————

I HAVE ALWAYS HAD A LOVE AND FASCINATION FOR THE ANCIENT holy days and their celebratory worship of God. Not only do they look to the past with gratitude, but they look to the future with hopeful anticipation of salvation through the Messiah. And thus, they have informed my own sense of gratitude for the past: for the gift of love from my Savior, Jesus Christ, who rescued and delivered me into the light of His gospel and Church. I also look with joyful anticipation for the day that the Messiah will show Himself in the heavens, and "take us to Him" to live with Him forever.

I am deeply grateful for my children, Lisa and Travis, who have always supported and encouraged me in the endeavor to share my studies and love of the scriptures with others. They eagerly participated in our Passover dinners, assisted with the preparations, and joined in the discussion of the "talk feast." They, also, love the many symbols and rituals that testify of the life and mission of the Messiah, Jesus Christ.

I am also grateful to Marilyn Springgay, a former English professor, who patiently reads through every chapter for editing. Her professional help, as well as her enthusiastic support, has been invaluable to me.

I also wish to thank B'Nai Shalom—Jews and Latter-day Saints, including Marlena Tanya Muchnick-Baker and her husband, Daniel Baker, for embracing me and encouraging me to write this book. I hope to build bridges of love and understanding between all the children of Abraham.

Other books by Lynda Cherry

The Redemption of the Bride:
God's Redeeming Love for His Covenant People

Judah and Joseph Reunited: The Hope for Israel

Contents

—◦◦◦—

Introduction: The Feasts and Festivals
  and Their Relevance to the Church 1

1. Temple-Centered Holy Days 5
2. Messiah-Centered Holy Days 11
3. Seven Feasts 15
4. The Law of Moses 17
5. The Spring Feasts 21
6. Out of Egypt 25
7. Symbols of the Passover, or *Pesach* 31
8. The Messiah Born at Passover 37
9. Jesus at Passover, *Pesach* 41
10. Jesus Christ: Lamb of God and Messiah 49
11. A Cup for Elijah 61
12. The Night of Watchings 65
13. The Lamb Is Slain 73
14. The Passover, *Seder*, or Order 89
15. Remarkable Passover Celebrations 103
16. The Feast of Unleavened Bread—*Hag HaMatzot* 105
17. Passover and Feast of Unleavened Bread Work Chart 107
18. The Feast of Firstfruits and The Savior:
    "The Firstfruits of Them Who Slept" 111
19. The Feast of Firstfruits and The Lord's Vineyard 119
20. Feast of Firstfruits, *Bikkurim*, Work Chart 127
21. Feast of Pentecost, *Shavuot* 131
22. Feast of Pentecost, *Shavuot:* The Gift of the Law 135

CONTENTS

23. Feast of Pentecost, *Shavuot*:
    The Betrothal of Jehovah to His People 139
24. The New and Everlasting Covenant—
    Invitation to a Covenant Fulness 145
25. Feast of Pentecost, *Shavuot*, Work Chart 153
26. The Feast of Trumpets, *Rosh Hashanah* 157
27. The Feast of Trumpets and The Book of Mormon 161
28. Feast of Trumpets Work Chart 165
29. The Day of Atonement, *Yom Kippur* 167
30. The Day of Atonement and Jesus Christ, the Messiah 177
31. The Day of Atonement, *Yom Kippur*, Work Chart 183
32. Feast of Tabernacles, *Sukkot* 187
33. Jesus at the Feast of Tabernacles 195
34. The Final Harvest, The Gathering of Israel 203
35. King Jesus and the *Hak'hel* Ceremony 211
36. The *Sukkah* Wedding *Chuppah*
    and the Marriage Supper of the Lord 217
37. Feast of Tabernacles, *Sukkot*, Work Chart 229

Conclusion 233
Bibliography 235
About the Author 239

Introduction

——— ❧ ———

The Feasts and Festivals and Their Relevance to the Church

*Behold, my soul delighteth in proving unto my people
the truth of the coming of Christ;
for, for this end hath the law of Moses been given:
and all things which have been given of God
from the beginning of the world, unto man,
are the typifying of Him.[1]*

WHAT ARE THE FEASTS AND FESTIVALS OF THE MESSIAH? AREN'T they just "Jewish holidays" that are defunct since the Law of Moses is fulfilled, and the Jerusalem temple destroyed?

When Jehovah, who is Jesus Christ, met with Moses at Mt. Sinai, He gave detailed instructions on the building of the tabernacle/temple and its services that included seven holy feast days, or convocations, to be kept by *all* the children of Israel. The timing, dates, sacrifices and rituals surrounding these feasts are explained in Leviticus 23, where the Lord includes the instruction that the feast days *"shall be a statute for ever in all your dwellings throughout your generations."*[2]

While the instruction to "keep" the feast days forever was given to all of Israel, only the Jews, as one of the distinct tribes of Israel, have continued to honor and celebrate them today. This is likely because most of the remaining tribes of Israel were assimilated into the countries that conquered them, and have lost the memory of their familial and covenantal roots.

Ezekiel prophesies of a restoration of the feast days during the Millennium,[3] and Zechariah specifically names the Feast of Tabernacles as a feast that will be kept and honored by *all* the nations of the earth during the Millennial reign of Christ.[4]

During the last few decades, Messianic Jews (Jews who believe Jesus, or Yeshua, is the Messiah) have brought more attention to the feast days, and a number of their websites are dedicated to the study of the festivals as symbolic of the mission of the Messiah. A quick scan through Amazon.com reveals that many Christian writers have also begun to show a keen interest in the ancient feasts and festivals, and their obvious connection to Jesus Christ.

However, The Church of Jesus Christ of Latter-day Saints may have a unique perspective in recognizing the prophetic nature of the feasts, and their fulfillment, not only in the Atonement of Jesus Christ, but also in the restoration of sacred doctrine and keys. Not only did Joseph Smith receive the plates of the Book of Mormon on the Feast of Trumpets, but the appearance of Elijah at the Kirtland Temple corresponded to the Passover promise of his return. The Book of Mormon, itself, reveals a people who honored and kept the ancient feast days, where King Benjamin followed the traditions of the Feast of Tabernacles,[5] and Alma appears to have followed the tradition of teaching his sons during the Passover ritual.[6]

When we recognize that the dates coincide with important events in Church history, and that the spring and fall feast days often overlap with the spring and fall General Conferences of the Church, we might regard these ancient temple celebrations with curiosity and interest.

Why does the Lord care so much about specific dates, and what are we to learn about the fact that He does?

What do the ancient feast and festival days teach us about the foreordained mission of the Savior, Jesus Christ? How can studying the feast days help us to have a greater appreciation for the sacrament—an ordinance that Jesus instituted during a Passover meal?

If the feast days are to be kept during the Millennium, as prophesied, how can we better understand their role in our worship? Can studying them help us to prepare for the Second Coming?

Lastly, as Israelites who were commanded to remember them forever, how can we teach our families about the feast days and help them recognize them as a further witness of God's great Plan of Salvation?

---

1 2 Nephi 11:4.
2 Leviticus 23:21.
3 See Ezekiel 45–46.
4 Zechariah 14:16.
5 See Mosiah 2–6.
6 See Alma 36–42.

CHAPTER 1

———⟨∞⟩———

Temple-Centered Holy Days

Three times in a year shall all thy males appear before the Lord God
in the place which he shall choose;
in the feast of unleavened bread,
and in the feast of weeks, and in the feast of tabernacles:
and they shall not appear before the Lord empty.[1]

WITH THE EXCEPTION OF THE FIRST PASSOVER, OR *PESACH*, IN Egypt, the seven feast days ordained by the Lord were to take place at the temple (or the tabernacle while in the wilderness). The Lord commanded that all males were to present themselves before the Lord "in the place which he shall choose"—or in other words, the temple. It was a serious and sacred appointment, where one was to consider his standing before God, receive more of His word, and to renew his covenants with Jehovah.

Sarah E. Fisher explained that the Hebrew word *moed* refers to an "appointed time" and "reflects the times that God has specifically appointed to honour and remember moments in history when God rescued his people. . . . These appointed times are holy, or set aside, because they are also times when God meets with us. He connects with us, on our level, during these feasts and festivals."[2]

The "three times in a year" referenced in the verse quoted at the beginning of this chapter encompassed all seven feasts, as three were celebrated in the spring (Passover or *Pesach*, Feast of Unleavened Bread or *Hag Ha-Matzot*, and Feast of Firstfruits or *Bikkurim*), one fifty days following Passover (Feast of Weeks or Pentecost or *Shavuot*), and three were celebrated in the fall (Feast of Trumpets or *Rosh Hashanah*, Day of Atonement or *Yom Kippur*, and Feast of Tabernacles or *Sukkot*).

The temple was the center of Israelite social life as well as its spiritual center. In addition to the daily sacrifices and the daily hour of prayer, the seven holy festivals kept the community focused on God, as they sang the psalms before Him, and participated in the sacred rituals.

The book of John focuses on the temple-centered feasts as a background to the ministry of Jesus. Almost all of the events recorded by John took place in Jerusalem in or near the temple, and during the feast day celebrations. The only chapters in John that do *not* reference a feast day are chapters 1 and 4. Jesus's greatest public declarations: "I am the living water,"[3] and "I am the light of the world"[4] took place at the temple during the Feast of Tabernacles. His statement "I am the bread of life" occurred in Galilee, but John places the Passover feast in context, by noting that Jesus and His disciples were shortly to make their way to the temple in Jerusalem as the Passover was near at hand.[5]

The Passover and the Feast of Unleavened Bread were celebrated together in the same week.[6] The bread held a central symbolic role in the Passover meal, and it was with the bread of the Passover meal that Jesus instituted the first sacrament, when He said: "Take, eat; this is my body,"[7] or as recorded in Luke, "This is my body which is given for you: this do in remembrance of me."[8] John is a deliberate witness of the fact that the rituals of the feasts and festivals testified of Jesus as the Messiah.

The book of Leviticus contains specific instructions regarding the seven feast or festival days, but it also records specifics for temple services and sacrifices. The *Old Testament Seminary Teacher Manual* queries: "Why study this book?" And then explains:

> The word *Leviticus* is a Latin word that has reference to the Levites—one of the twelve tribes of Israel. The Levites held the lesser priesthood and were given the responsibility to officiate in the tabernacle and later at the temple in Jerusalem.[9] The book of Leviticus contains instructions on performing priesthood duties, such as animal sacrifice and other rituals that would help teach the children of Israel about Jesus Christ and His Atonement.[10] The Lord

revealed a primary purpose for the instructions He gave in the book of Leviticus: "Ye shall be holy: for I the Lord your God am holy."[11] As students study this book, they can deepen their understanding and appreciation of the Savior's Atonement. Students can also learn important truths that will help them to be holy, meaning spiritually clean and set apart for sacred purposes. Living these truths will prepare students to serve Heavenly Father and His children.[12]

If Israel were to become a "kingdom of priests" as promised in the Mt. Sinai covenant,[13] the place to begin their instruction was with the book of Leviticus.

The book of Leviticus is one of the most overlooked in the Bible. Yet, the training of Jewish children *began* with the book of Leviticus.[14] Alfred Edersheim explained that:

As soon as the child had any knowledge, the private and the united prayers of the family, and the domestic rites, whether of the weekly Sabbath or of festive seasons, would indelibly impress themselves upon his mind. It would be difficult to say which of those feasts would have the most vivid effect upon a child's imagination ... From the moment a child was at all capable of being instructed— still more, of his taking any part in the services— the impression would deepen day by day. Surely no one who had ever worshipped within the courts of Jehovah's house at Jerusalem could ever have forgotten the scenes he had witnessed, or the words he had heard. Standing in that gorgeous, glorious building, and looking up its terraced vista, the child would watch with solemn awe, not unmingled with wonderment, as the great throng of white-robed priests busily moved about, while the smoke of the sacrifice rose from the altar of burnt-offering. Then, amid the hushed silence of that vast multitude, they had all fallen down to worship at the time of incense. Again, on those steps that led up to the innermost sanctuary the priests had lifted their hands and spoken over the people the words of blessing; and then, while the drink-offering was poured out, the Levites' chant of Psalms had risen and swelled into a mighty volume ... The Jewish child knew many of these words. They had been the earliest songs he had heard ... But now, in those white-marbled, gold-adorned halls, under heaven's blue canopy, and with such surroundings, they would fall upon his ear like sounds from another world, to which the prolonged threefold blasts from the silver trumpets of the priests would seem to waken him. And *they were* sounds from another world; for, as his father would tell him, all that he saw was after the exact pattern of heavenly things which God had shown to Moses on Mount Sinai; all that he heard was God-uttered, spoken by Jehovah Himself through the mouth of His servant David, and of the other sweet singers of Israel . . . Verily this Temple with its services was heaven upon earth![15]

The city of Jerusalem has been called "the navel of the earth" for thousands of years. It is the holy city for Israelites, Jews, Muslims, and Christians. Within that holy city, lies its heart, the temple mount. An article in *The Jerusalem Post* asserted: "Jerusalem has but one center of gravity, known as axis mundi or 'the navel of the world.' This place is called 'the Temple Mount'—with the definite article."[16]

The Jerusalem temple was destroyed twice, first by the Babylonian conquest in 587/586 BC and the second temple was destroyed by the Romans in 70 AD.

Following the Babylonian conquest, more Jews lived outside of Israel than within it. This situation is referred to as the *Diaspora*, or the dispersion. After the second temple was built, these dispersed Jewish people made a pilgrimage to Jerusalem for the feast days. Josephus, an ancient historian contemporary with the Gospel authors, stated that at Passover, the population of Jerusalem swelled to over two million, and necessitated the sacrifice of 256,500 lambs.[17] Although some have disputed Josephus's numbers, they give us an idea as to how seriously the Jewish pilgrims took the command to present themselves on these holy days before the Lord in Jerusalem.

Once the temple was destroyed again in 70 AD the sacrifices at the temple ceased, but the Jewish people (mostly) continued to celebrate the non-sacrificial rituals of the feast days in their homes and communities. For many, the feast days are still a time of sacred remembrance and renewal.

Maimonides stated: "Even though, the Temple is now in ruin because of our sins, a person must hold its [site] in awe, as one would regard it when it was standing."[18]

---

1 Deuteronomy 16:16.

2 Fisher, "Moed: The Creator's Appointed Times," *Hebrew Word Lessons*.

3 John 7:37.

4 John 8:12.

5 See John 6:4, 35.

6 See Luke 7:7.

7 Matthew 26:26.

8 Luke 22:19.

9 See Numbers 3:5–10.

10 See Alma 34:13–14.

11 Leviticus 19:2; see also Leviticus 11:44–45; 20:25; 21:6.

12 "Introduction to Leviticus," *Old Testament Seminary Teacher Manual*.

13 See Exodus 19:5–6.

14 Edersheim, *The Life and Times of Jesus the Messiah*, 161.

15 Edersheim, *Sketches of a Jewish Social Life*, 103–4.

16 Shana, "A glimpse into the 'navel of the world,'" *The Jerusalem Post*.

17 Josephus, *War 6.9.3*, 422–27.

18 *Beit Haberchirah*, 6:7.

CHAPTER 2

Messiah-Centered Holy Days

And behold, this is the whole meaning of the law,
every whit pointing to that great and last sacrifice;
and that great and last sacrifice
will be the Son of God, yea, infinite and eternal.[1]

As we glance through the chapters of Leviticus, we see that Jehovah Himself gave instructions as to how He was to be worshipped. We see detailed information about how sacrifices were to be prepared and offered. We note that sacrifices varied on the different festival days, and that the mood could change from serious reflection during the Day of Atonement, to rejoicing and celebration at the Feast of Tabernacles. There was the golden pitcher of water at the Feast of Tabernacles, and the solemn assembly and the presentation of the family lamb at Passover. Throngs joined together to sing the Hallel, and the Levites blew their trumpets in joyful praise. It was a communal family bonded by covenant in the name of their God, Jehovah.

In all of these sacrifices and rituals, we see symbols that point to the mission and Atonement of the Savior. Amulek testified:

Therefore, it is expedient that there should be a great and last sacrifice,
and then shall there be, or it is expedient there should be,
a stop to the shedding of blood;
then shall the law of Moses be fulfilled;
yea, it shall be all fulfilled, every jot and tittle,

and none shall have passed away.
And behold, this is the whole meaning of the law,
every whit pointing to that great and last sacrifice;
and that great and last sacrifice will be the Son of God,
yea, infinite and eternal.[2]

One writer notes:

The first point, then, which requires our notice is this: In each offering there are at least *three distinct objects* presented to us. There is the *offering*, the *priest*, the *offerer*. A definite knowledge of the precise import of each of these is absolutely requisite if we would understand the offerings. What, then, is the *offering*? What the *priest*? What the *offerer*? Christ is the offering; Christ is the priest; Christ is the offerer. Such and so manifold are the relations in which Christ has stood for man and to man, that no one type or set of types can adequately represent the fulness of them . . . As man under the law, our substitute, Christ stood for us towards God as offerer . . . Thus His body was His offering: he willingly offered it; and then as priest He took the blood into the holiest. As *offerer*, we see Him *man under the law*, standing our substitute, for us to fulfill all righteousness. As *priest*, we have Him presented as the *mediator*, God's messenger between Himself and Israel. While as the *offering* He is seen *the innocent victim*, a sweet savor to God, yet bearing the sin and dying for it.[3]

Jesus and His apostles kept and honored the feasts more than a thousand years after Moses. It was during Passover that Jesus, at twelve years old, left his parents' side, to return to the temple.[4] It was at Passover that Jesus first overturned the moneychangers' tables at the temple and declared that it was His "Father's house,"[5] and Passover again, when He overthrew the tables a second time, declaring this time that the temple was *His* house.[6] It was at Passover that Jesus performed the Atonement, gave up His life, and was placed in the tomb. He arose from the dead on the Feast of Firstfruits, or *Bikkurim*.

Jesus Christ, Jehovah, Yahweh, Yeshua, is at the heart of the temple, its services, and its feast days.

Paul explained that the holy feast days were "a shadow of things to come," and that they testified of Jesus as the Christ and the long-awaited Messiah.[7]

Edward Chumney states, "Although God gave us festivals to observe, God never gave the festivals so we would obtain salvation from Him by observing them because salvation only comes by faith (*emunah*); however God did give the festivals for the purpose of teaching and instructing His people concerning His plan of redemption and our personal relationship to Him."[8]

The timing of the spring and fall feasts fall into natural order for an agriculturally-based people, who planted in the spring and brought in the harvest in the fall. Even as the animal sacrifices testified of Him, these high holy days typify the first and second comings of the Messiah, Jesus Christ. In the spring Passover of His birth, ministry, death, and resurrection, He planted the seed of His gospel, watered that seed with His blood, and promised to return again for the fall harvest, culminating in the Feast of Tabernacles, often referred to as the Feast of the Bridegroom.

> *Then shall we know, if we follow on to know the Lord:*
> *his going forth is prepared as the morning;*
> *and he shall come unto us as the rain,*
> *as the latter and former rain unto the earth.[9]*

In the above verse in Hosea 6:3, some believe they see prophetic evidence of *two* visits by the Messiah.[10] The rains came to Israel in the spring and the fall, as did the festival days. His first visit did take place in the spring. Will His second coming take place in the fall? In either case, it is a beautiful image to think of the coming of the Savior as rain to a desert!

Gale T. Boyd writes:

Rabbi Eliezer, seeing Messianic imagery in the holidays, came to the conclusion that the Messiah would come to redeem Israel during the month of *Nisan* in the spring. Rabbi Joshua disagreed with him. Surely, he said, the Messiah would come in *Tishri*—the imagery of the fall holidays proves it. We know that both Rabbis were correct. These months are the meridians of the civil and religious Jewish year. The Passover in the month of *Nisan* testifies of the birth, life, mission, crucifixion and resurrection of the Savior. The fall holidays in the month of *Tishri* testify of his second coming. One might ask, then, can't we expect the Second Coming to occur in the fall? Not exactly. We know that Christ will make several appearances which will all be a part of the Second Coming. The event where he again partakes of the bread and wine, together with his Chosen, is a Passover fulfillment, yet it will be a Second Coming event. The imagery is what is important, and not so much the exact timing. Rest assured, the pieces will fit together tightly and exactly; every type will be fulfilled as promised. However, the entire puzzle will not be clear to us until it is finished.[11]

---

1 Alma 34:14.
2 Alma 34:13–14.
3 Jukes, *The Law of the Offerings*, 44–45, emphasis added.
4 Luke 2:46; see Joseph Smith Translation.
5 John 2:16.
6 Matthew 21:13.
7 Colossians 2:16–17.
8 Chumney, *The Seven Festivals of the Messiah*, 5.
9 Hosea 6:3.
10 See Chumney, *The Seven Festivals of the Messiah*, 9.
11 Boyd, *Days of Awe*, 120.

CHAPTER 3

―――――― ✺ ――――――

Seven Feasts

And the Lord spake unto Moses, saying,
Speak unto the children of Israel, and say unto them,
concerning the feasts of the Lord,
which ye shall proclaim to be holy convocations,
even these are my feasts . . .
In the fourteenth day of the first month
*at even is the Lord's **Passover.***
And on the fifteenth day of the same month
*is the **feast of unleavened bread** unto the Lord:*
seven days ye must eat unleavened bread . . .
then ye shall bring a sheaf
*of the **first fruits** of your harvest unto the priest;*
and he shall wave the sheaf before the Lord . . .
it shall be a statute for ever
through your generations in all your dwellings.

And ye shall count you from the morrow after the sabbath,
from the day that ye brought the sheaf of the wave offering;
*seven sabbaths . . . ye shall number fifty days . . . [**Pentecost**].¹*

In the seventh month, in the first day of the month,
shall ye have a sabbath,
*a memorial of blowing of **trumpets**, an holy convocation. . . .*
Also on the tenth day of this seventh month
*there shall be a **day of atonement**:*
it shall be a holy convocation unto you . . .
[and] the fifteenth day of this seventh month
*shall be the **feast of tabernacles** for seven days unto the Lord. . . .*
It shall be a statute forever in your generations.²

THE SPRING FESTIVALS, REPRESENTING THE FIRST COMING OF our Lord, are: Passover (*Pesach*), Feast of Unleavened Bread (*Hag HaMatzah*), and the Feast of First Fruits (*Bikkurim*). The fall festivals, representing the second coming of the Savior, are: Feast of Trumpets (*Rosh Hashanah*), Day of Atonement (*Yom Kippur*), and Feast of Tabernacles (*Sukkot*). The "middle" feast is Pentecost, or *Shavout*, celebrating the reception of the Law at Sinai.

For our purposes, we will only be studying the seven feasts ordained at Mt. Sinai, and not the "new" feasts of Purim or Hanukkah.

Alfred Edersheim wrote:

> The symbolical character which is to be traced in all the institutions of the Old Testament, appears also in the arrangement of its festive calendar. Whatever classification of the festivals may be proposed, one general characteristic pervades the whole.
>
> Unquestionably, the number *seven* marks in Scripture the sacred measurement of time. The Sabbath is the seventh of days; seven weeks after the commencement of the ecclesiastical year is the Feast of Pentecost; the seventh month is more sacred than the rest ... Similarly, each seventh year is Sabbatical, and after seven times seven years comes that of Jubilee."[3]

The dates for the feast days are determined by the Jewish lunar calendar, and vary from year to year.

Gale Boyd explains: "The Jewish calendar is a 'luni-solar' calendar. The months are based on the phases of the moon (beginning with new moons), and they have an average length of 29.5 days. The Jewish year usually contains twelve months (about 354 days). The calendar has a nineteen year cycle with leap years on the third, sixth, eighth, eleventh, fourteenth, seventeenth, and nineteenth years. During leap years one extra day is added to the month of *Adar*, and a thirteenth month (*Adar sheni*) is added to the calendar. This lunar reckoning causes the holidays to fall on different dates each year (that is, on *our* calendar), yet to stay in the same season."[4]

---

1 Leviticus 23:1–16.
2 Leviticus 23:24–34, 41.
3 Edersheim, *The Temple: Its Ministry and Services*, 151–52.
4 Boyd, *Days of Awe*, 38.

CHAPTER 4

———⌒◇⌒———

The Law of Moses

Think not that I am come to destroy the law, or the prophets:
I am not come to destroy, but to fulfill.[1]

THE ANCIENT TEMPLE SERVICES AND THE FEAST DAY OBSERVANCES
were all decreed under the Law of Moses. Many seem to look
at anything to do with the Law of Moses with suspicion, as if the
Law of Moses were intended for lesser mortals who just didn't "get
it." However, upon reflection, we may learn to view the Law as the
Israelites did: as a gift of the covenant given by the Lord.

Judaism 101 says this of the Law: "When you do these things, you
are constantly reminded of your relationship with the Divine, and it
becomes an integral part of your entire existence."[2]

Nephi stated that when he and his brothers obtained the brass
plates, on which was recorded "the Law and the Prophets," they
"searched them and found that they were desirable; yea, even of great
worth unto us . . ."[3]

Many teach and believe that when Jesus said, "in me is the law
of Moses fulfilled,"[4] He meant that the Law of Moses had become a
dead thing.

Jesus said:

For behold, the covenant which I have made
with my people is not all fulfilled;
but the law which was given unto Moses hath an end in me.[5]

The way we use the word "end" today might lead us to see that sentence as saying something like "the Law of Moses is over." Yet, Jesus used the same word, "end," in this manner to Pilate:

> *To this end was I born,*
> *and for this cause came I into the world.*[6]

In this case, Jesus is saying to Pilate: "for this *purpose* was I born" . . . could the same application be given to the 3 Nephi statement, "the law which was given unto Moses hath its *purpose* in me"?

Jesus said:

> *Think not that I am come to destroy the law, or the prophets:*
> *I am not come to destroy, but to fulfill.*
> *For verily I say unto you, Till heaven and earth pass,*
> *one jot or one tittle shall in no wise pass from the law,*
> *till all be fulfilled.*[7]

This debate is not easily settled. Which parts of the Law of Moses do we think are "done away with"? Most people will quickly answer, "circumcision!" because we know that circumcision was specifically debated amongst the Apostles in the early church[8]—however, circumcision was not a Law of Moses practice, but began with Abraham.

Nothing symbolizes the Law of Moses more than the Ten Commandments, which were written on stone tablets by the finger of God. Are the Ten Commandments obsolete? Are the two greatest laws to "love God with all one's heart, might, mind and strength, and to love one's neighbor as one's self" done away with?[9] Jesus said "On these two commandments hang all the law and the prophets."[10]

Certainly, the law of blood sacrifice must be "fulfilled" and "ended" with the Atonement of Jesus Christ—and, yet, we know through modern prophecy that blood sacrifice will again be enacted in a future day.[11] Joseph Smith taught:

> It is generally supposed that sacrifice was entirely done away when the Great Sacrifice [i.e., the sacrifice of the Lord Jesus] was offered up, and that there will be no necessity for the ordinance of sacrifice in the future; but those who assert this are certainly not acquainted with the duties, privileges and authority of the priesthood, or with the Prophets.

The offering of sacrifice has ever been connected and forms a part of the duties of the Priesthood. It began with the Priesthood, and will be continued until after the coming of Christ, from generation to generation. . . .

These sacrifices, as well as every ordinance belonging to the Priesthood, will, when the Temple of the Lord shall be built, and the sons of Levi be purified, be fully restored and attended to in all their powers, ramifications, and blessings. This ever did and ever will exist when the powers of the Melchizedek Priesthood are sufficiently manifest; else how can the restitution of all things spoken of by the holy Prophets be brought to pass. It is not to be understood that the law of Moses will be established again with all its rites and variety of ceremonies; this has never been spoken of by the prophets: but those things which existed prior to Moses' day, namely, sacrifice, will be continued.[12]

Hopefully, we recognize that we don't have a full understanding of the Law of Moses, nor of the specific aspects that are defunct. The prophecies of Ezekiel and Zechariah[13] that testify of future feast-day celebrations, together with Joseph Smith's teaching on blood sacrifice, indicate that we should perhaps be prepared to see some aspects of the Law of Moses in the future. In the meantime, we can learn much about the Messiah and the covenant by studying the Law and its practices, and allowing the Spirit to teach us what is most meaningful to our lives and understanding.

---

1 Matthew 5:17.
2 Rich, "Halakhah: Jewish Law," *Judaism 101.*
3 1 Nephi 5:21.
4 3 Nephi 9:17.
5 3 Nephi 15:8.
6 John 18:37.
7 Matthew 5:17–18
8 See Acts 15.
9 See Leviticus 19:18; Matthew 22:36–40.
10 Matthew 22:40.
11 See Doctrine and Covenants 13.
12 *Teachings of the Prophet Joseph Smith,* 172–73.
13 Ezekiel 45:21; Zechariah 14:16.

CHAPTER 5

The Spring Feasts

Speak unto the children of Israel, and say unto them,
concerning the feasts of the Lord,
which ye shall proclaim to be holy convocations,
even these are my feasts. . . .These are the feasts
of the Lord, even holy convocations,
which ye shall proclaim in their seasons.
*In the fourteenth day of the first month at even is the Lord's **passover**.*
And on the fifteenth day of the same month
*is the feast of **unleavened bread** unto the Lord:*
seven days ye must eat unleavened bread.
In the first day ye shall have an holy convocation:
ye shall do no servile work therein.
But ye shall offer an offering made by fire unto the Lord seven days:
in the seventh day is an holy convocation:
ye shall do no servile work therein.
And the Lord spake unto Moses, saying,
speak unto the children of Israel, and say unto them,
When ye be come into the land which I give unto you,
and shall reap the harvest thereof,
*then ye shall bring a sheaf of the **firstfruits** of your harvest unto the priest:*
and he shall wave the sheaf before the Lord, to be accepted for you:
on the morrow after the sabbath the priest shall wave it.
And ye shall offer that day when ye wave the sheaf
an he lamb without blemish of the first year
for a burnt offering unto the Lord.

And the meat offering thereof
shall be two tenth deals of fine flour mingled with oil,
an offering made by fire unto the Lord for a sweet savor:
and the drink offering thereof shall be of wine, the fourth part of an hin.
And ye shall eat neither bread, nor parched corn, nor green ears,
until the selfsame day that ye have brought an offering unto your God:
it shall be a statute for ever
throughout your generations in all your dwellings.[1]

THE PASSOVER, OR *PESACH,* MARKED THE BEGINNING OF A NEW religious year and the first of the spring feasts, or holy days, for the Israelites. As noted in Leviticus above, the Passover takes place on the 14th of Nisan, the Feast of Unleavened Bread on the 15th (for seven days), and the Feast of Firstfruits is the day after the weekly Sabbath (a Sunday).

The first Passover, with the lamb's blood marking the homes of those that the angel of death would "pass over" and the consequent miraculous deliverance of the children of Israel out of Egypt, through the Red Sea, and into the presence of Jehovah at Sinai was to be memorialized forever. Miraculous though it was in and of itself, it was to be a type or foreshadowing of an even greater miracle—the individual deliverance, redemption, and salvation of every living soul through the atoning sacrifice of the Lamb of God, Jesus Christ.

The Passover, The Feast of Unleavened Bread, and the Feast of Firstfruits with their manifold symbols, reveal layer upon layer of possible interpretation. All of them point to Jesus as Messiah, the Redeemer of Israel. But there is personal application, as well, for each one of us. Will we choose the Lamb, as ritual dictates, and bring Him into our homes? Will we seek the Christ, Who is hidden from the world's unseeing eyes, and will we apply His blood to the doorposts of our heart?

One of the beauties of participating in ritual *feasting* is the opportunity to ponder and reflect upon the meaning of each act, each symbol, and to seek personal inspiration for their application to our lives. The ancient Israelites had that opportunity as they celebrated the feasts of the Lord, and we also have that opportunity as we partake of the feast of the sacrament table each sabbath, or participate in the sacred rituals of the temple.

Because there are so many symbols associated with the spring feasts, it is not really possible to provide all of the possible meanings and interpretations in this writing. We can only highlight a few, with the hope that the Spirit will reveal more to each reader, according to his/her desire.

The spring feasts testify of Jesus Christ as Messiah, and many believe that they specifically witness of His "first" coming, or of His atonement, death, and resurrection. These symbols of the feast testify of God's love for His people, and His absolute commitment to the covenant promises He has made with mothers and fathers throughout time, starting with Adam and Eve. The name that the Lord has given to His covenant family is *Israel*, and all are invited to become a part of that family, regardless of their heritage, race, color, or gender. The first Passover and its exodus tells the story of the birth of Israel as a nation, and their progress to the promised land.

Noted scholar, Alfred Edersheim explains:

> Thus *nature, history*, and *grace* combined to give a special meaning to the festivals, but chiefly to the Passover. It was the feast of spring; the springtime of nature, when, after the death of winter, the scattered seeds were born into a new harvest, and the first ripe sheaf could be presented to the Lord; the springtime of Israel's history, too, when each year the people celebrated anew their national birthday; and the spring-time of grace, their grand national deliverance pointing forward to the birth of the true Israel, and the Passover sacrifice to that "Lamb of God which taketh away the sin of the world." Accordingly, the month of the Passover, Abib, or, as it was called in later times, Nisan, was to be unto them "the beginning of months"—the birth-month of the sacred . . ..[2]

---

1 Leviticus 23:2–14, emphasis added.
2 Edersheim, *The Temple, Its Ministry and Services*, 163–64.

CHAPTER 6

Out of Egypt

For I will pass through the land of Egypt this night,
and will smite all the firstborn in the land of Egypt,
both man and beast;
and against all the gods of Egypt
I will execute judgment: I am the Lord.
And the blood shall be to you for a token
upon the houses where ye are:
and when I see the blood, I will pass over you,
and the plague shall not be upon you to destroy you,
when I smite the land of Egypt.
And this day shall be unto you for a memorial;
and ye shall keep it a feast to the Lord throughout your generations;
ye shall keep it a feast by an ordinance for ever.[1]

EGYPT WAS GLUTTED WITH IDOLS AND GODS. MAMMOTH PYRA-
mids, obelisks, and statues reflected the Egyptian fascination with
the afterlife, and their superstitious response to the teachings of their
priests. When Egypt went to battle against neighboring countries,
they called upon their gods for success. Priests and soothsayers would
"divine" the most propitious times for battles to be fought by using
star charts, and by reading the entrails of animals. Victory was proof
that one god was mightier than another, and Egypt reigned supreme
in world power, as did her gods. The sheer size of the country, the rich-
ness of its Nile-fed soil, the number of its slaves, and the opulence of its
palaces intimidated the surrounding nations. Careful record-keepers,
the Egyptians had carved their victories in stone for all to see; the captives they had conquered were recorded by number, the details of the

battles drawn and etched to last for millennia. No wonder Pharaoh taunted Moses: "Who is the Lord that I should obey his voice to let Israel go? I know not the Lord, neither will I let Israel go."[2]

Pharaoh's attitude prevails again in our day. People ask: "Who is Jesus Christ that I should submit or conform my life to His teachings?" When believers use the Lord's word to defend the family, for example, they are laughed to scorn. Just as with ancient Egypt, our land is full of man-made gods and idols; false priests teach soothing messages, and the pride of the people waxes strong. When calamity hits, rather than turning to God, mankind runs to their current pharaohs to solve their dilemma. Debate over who they will have to govern them leads people to question whether the name of God should be taken out of the American Pledge of Allegiance, for man has made himself his own god, and bows to no one.

Notwithstanding Pharaoh's lack of belief, or today's open attack against Christian principles, God's ability to carry out His work is not dependent upon the number of people who believe He can. The deliverance of the children of Israel was not performed in an attempt to convert Pharaoh, or even because of the righteousness of the delivered, but to keep a promise made to Abraham and Joseph.[3]

Even as He was making the initial covenant with Abraham, the Lord foretold:

Know of a surety that thy seed
shall be a stranger in a land that is not theirs,
and shall serve them;
and they shall afflict them four hundred years;
And also that nation, whom they shall serve, will I judge:
and afterward shall they come out with great substance.[4]

After the Israelites had become slaves in Egypt for an extended period,

. . . the children of Israel sighed by reason of the bondage,
and they cried,
and their cry came up unto God by reason of the bondage.
And God heard their groaning,
and God remembered his covenant
with Abraham, with Isaac, and with Jacob.

26

And God looked upon the children of Israel,
and God had respect unto them.[5]

It should be very reassuring to us to realize the determination with which God honors His promises. Other than Moses's family, who still adhered to their covenant-beliefs, we do not know the background of any other Israelite family in Egypt. We don't know how much they may have assimilated the Egyptian religions, and whether or not they still understood their relationship to Jehovah. We know that they doubted Moses, that they grumbled and groaned, and that they readily worshipped a golden calf at Sinai. However, the Lord reached out to save and deliver them, and extended the covenant promise to all of them because He had promised Abraham that He would. As children of Adam and Eve, with whom He also made covenants, and as adopted children of Abraham and Sarah, we can also take comfort in knowing that we are within God's plan of redemption.

Even Moses had his doubts that Pharaoh would ever release the Israelites from bondage. He had grown up in the Egyptian court, and knew its power. Pharaoh was considered a god amongst the people, and even believed it himself. Moses was clearly afraid of going before the king, and despite the assurances the Lord provided him, Moses still shrank back.[6] But, Moses grew in his faith and trust as he moved forward with the mission the Lord had called him to perform.

Deliverance—and faith—did not come immediately. The burdens became even greater for the children of Israel after Moses and Aaron spoke to Pharaoh.[7] Because of their painful circumstances, the Israelites were uncertain about Moses's role, and the way he stirred the pharaoh up in anger against them. They, like Pharaoh, did not believe that the Lord had power to deliver them.[8]

While we sojourn in this "foreign land" of the world, do we dwindle in unbelief, and doubt the Lord's power or reality? Will the burdens become greater today for those who stand for the word of the Lord? What will our reaction be if they do?

When Moses performed miracles in the name of the Lord, Pharaoh's wisemen and sorcerers could at first also perform similar miracles.[9] This undoubtedly caused confusion. Even as the false priests tried to "compete" with Moses, the outcome of this "competition" was known to the Lord *before Moses even left Sinai for Egypt*. The Lord knew which stroke would bring freedom. He instructed Moses:

And the Lord said unto Moses, When thou goest to return into Egypt,
see that thou do all those wonders before Pharaoh,
which I have put in thine hand . . .
And thou shalt say unto Pharaoh, Thus saith the Lord,
Israel is my son, even my firstborn:
And I say unto thee, Let my son go, that he may serve me:
and if thou refuse to let him go,
behold, I will slay thy son, even thy firstborn.[10]

The plagues the Lord poured out upon the Egyptians in order to persuade them to release the Israelites increased in their intensity. Each was ignored. But the final blow, the death of every firstborn male—man and beast—including the pharoah's son, was unbearable. Finally, overwhelmed with grief and anger, Pharaoh consented to let the Israelites leave Egypt . . . and then, he changed his mind.[11]

The death of the firstborn son had brought freedom. Jehovah had referred to Israel as His own firstborn son, and Israel was about to be born anew as a nation and as a covenant people, as they passed through their bloody doorposts, the waters of the Red Sea, and experienced the fiery pillar of the Lord as He led them to Mt. Sinai.

Yet, all that transpired foreshadowed and pointed towards the atoning life and death of Jesus Christ, the Firstborn Son of the Eternal Father. His was a life and death offered freely, yet at a terrible cost, in the hope that all who would partake of it might become sons and daughters of God through covenant, and find eternal life.

When Israel was a child, then I loved him,
and called my son out of Egypt.[12]

Israel, the "firstborn" nation unto God was being called out of Egypt to finally inherit the land promised to Abraham and Sarah. To add interest to the story, this foreshadowed the calling of Jesus as a child to also come out of Egypt. Matthew wrote:

And . . . behold, the angel of the Lord appeareth
to Joseph in a dream, saying,

Arise, and take the young child and his mother,
and flee into Egypt,
and be thou there until I bring thee word:
for Herod will seek the young child to destroy him.
When he arose, he took the young child
and his mother by night, and departed into Egypt:
and was there until the death of Herod:
that it might be fulfilled
which was spoken of the Lord by the prophet, saying,
Out of Egypt have I called my son.[13]

Jesus Christ, Jehovah, has given His life that we might escape our "Egypt," the harsh and enticing world in which we live and sometimes find ourselves in bondage. Will we accept His deliverance, or will be tempted to maintain a "summer cottage in Babylon" as Neal A. Maxwell once quipped?[14] We might realize that in order to really know God, we like the Israelites, will need to make the trek from Egypt to Sinai, leaving the bustling crowds behind us as we seek the mountain heights of revelation.

---

1 Exodus 12:12–14.
2 Exodus 5:2.
3 Genesis 15:13–16; Genesis 50:27–29 Joseph Smith Translation.
4 Genesis 15:13–14.
5 Exodus 2:23–25.
6 See Exodus 4.
7 Exodus 5:7–19.
8 Exodus 6:9.
9 Exodus 7:11, 22; 8:7.
10 Exodus 4:21–23.
11 See Exodus 12:29–32; 14:5–9.
12 Hosea 11:1.
13 Matthew 2:13–15.
14 Maxwell, *The Neal A. Maxwell Quote Book*, 25.

CHAPTER 7

Symbols of the Passover, or *Pesach*

Then Moses called for all the elders of Israel,
and said unto them,
Draw out and take you a lamb according to your families,
and kill the passover.
And ye shall take a bunch of hyssop,
and dip it in the blood that is in the basin,
and strike the lintel and the two side posts
with the blood that is in the basin;
and none of you shall go out
at the door of his house until the morning.
For the Lord will pass through to smite the Egyptians;
and when he seeth the blood upon the lintel,
and on the two side posts,
the Lord will pass over the door,
and will not suffer the destroyer
to come into your houses to smite you.
And ye shall observe this thing as an ordinance
to thee and to thy sons for ever.[1]
. . . For even Christ our passover is sacrificed for us.[2]

"THE LORD'S PASSOVER"[3] IS AN EVENT RICH IN SPIRITUAL SYM-bolism. It celebrates an occasion beyond parallel in history, when the Lord miraculously saved an entire population and delivered them from bondage. Prophets and faithful descendants have been referring to it throughout the ages, and most Jews celebrate and remember it today (Jews are the remaining tribe of Israel who clearly identify themselves as Israelites). It is meaningful for us, also, to study its symbols and to look for significance in our own lives. The Savior used the Passover meal as His Last Supper, implementing the tokens of the feast in the first sacrament.

Terry W. Treseder wrote:

The Last Supper was not only outstanding as a new sacrament. It was also the fulfillment of more than a thousand years of promises repeated and prayed for every year during the Passover service since the days of Israel's wandering in the wilderness. The more we understand and appreciate the Passover service as the Jews observed it in Jesus's day, the more deeply we can understand our sacramental covenants and marvel anew at the infinite love and sacrifice of our Brother, the Lord Jesus Christ.[4]

Gayle Boyd noted:

Why repeat this teaching exercise [of the Passover] over and over? Because in the pattern and story of the Passover and the Exodus, is found the type of the life, mission, and redemptive power of the Savior, and the spiritual history of the earth. Not until the End of Times will the full import of the imagery fall into place.[5]

The *Old Testament Student Manual* says:

Look for the Savior in the symbols and imagery of the scriptures. Since Jesus Christ and His atoning sacrifice are the central and most fundamental part of the Latter-day Saint religion, it is not surprising that virtually all scriptural symbols are Christ-centered. One could say that all of the parables, every simile, each metaphor, and all of the types are designed to teach the children of God what they must do to incorporate the infinite sacrifice of Christ into their own life. . . . Nephi taught the all-embracing pervasiveness of scriptural symbolism when he said, "Behold, my soul delighteth in proving unto my people the truth of the coming of Christ; for, for this end hath the law of Moses been given; and all things which have been given of God from the beginning of the world are the typifying of him" (2 Nephi 11:4; emphasis added).[6]

A note about the Passover Seder *Haggadah* or "storytelling." There are more than 2,000 different Passover Seder texts. They continue to evolve and to change to fit the desires of those who celebrate it. The Seder text is passed down from generation to generation in an attempt to unify and bond the covenant people, as they are reminded of their heritage and of the deliverance and redemption that God has provided for them as a people. The word "Seder" means *order*. We do not know the "order" that was followed at the time of Christ, and the word *Seder* would not have been used. Whether the Savior, as Host, followed the specific order used today is unknown, but there is evidence that foundations of the *order* as we know it were present in His last Passover supper: the blessing of the cup(s), the washing of the Apostles' feet, the giving of the sop to Judas, the blessing and breaking of the bread, the emphasis on the cup of Redemption, and the singing of the Hallel have been recorded by the Gospel authors as having occurred at the last meal Jesus shared with His apostles.

The following is a list of instructions and symbols pertaining to "the Lord's Passover." Ponder each one, and contemplate the thoughts and images that come to your mind and heart. Each symbol has many layers; you may focus on one now, but discover another later. We will discuss them in greater detail as we progress. While there are many interpretations provided by scholars and historians, it is particularly important to allow the spirit of revelation to speak directly to your own heart, which is why this list is placed here, before we read explanations or definitions provided by others. At the end of the section on each feast, there will be a chart where some interpretations are suggested, but also where you can write in your own personal insights.

- The day of Passover was to become a *"beginning of months"* or a new year.[7] The Israelites were to celebrate two new years—the second was during the fall feasts, at the Feast of Trumpets. The new year at Passover was considered a spiritual, or religiously based new year.
- The lamb for the Passover sacrifice was to be chosen *on the tenth day* of the month.[8]
- There was to be one lamb for each household or a certain "number of souls."[9]
- The lamb should be without blemish, a male of the first year.[10]
- The lamb was to be killed *on the fourteenth day.*[11]

- Each household was to mark the *upper and side posts* of the house with the blood with a hyssop branch.[12]
- The lamb was to be roasted with fire.[13]
- Not a bone of the lamb was to be broken.[14]
- The Passover was to be eaten with unleavened bread (unleavened bread was to be eaten for seven days).[15]
- The Passover lamb was to be eaten with bitter herbs.[16]
- The whole lamb was to be roasted and completely eaten—no leftovers.[17]
- Four cups of wine, each with its own name, are used to commemorate the Lord's promises. The names and the promise are taken from the Lord's own words:

> *Wherefore say unto the children of Israel,*
> *I am the Lord, and* ***I will bring you out***
> *from under the burdens of the Egyptians,*
> *and* ***I will rid you out of their bondage***,
> *and* ***I will redeem you*** *with a stretched out arm,*
> *and with great judgments:*
> *And* ***I will take you to me*** *for a people,*
> *and I will be to you a God:*
> *and ye shall know that I am the Lord your God,*
> *which bringeth you out from under the burdens of the Egyptians.*[18]

Each cup is called by its name, and savored at various points of the Passover ritual. One does not sip from each cup, but is instructed to drink it completely and to finish each one before proceeding further. The cups are called:

1) I Will Bring You Out
2) I Will Deliver You
3) I Will Redeem You
4) I Will Take You to Me

- The first Passover was to be eaten with loins girded and shoes on the feet and staff in hand; eaten in haste.[19]
- It is *the Lord's Passover.*[20] He gave the particulars as to how it was to be kept.

- A holy convocation, or sabbath, should be for the first and last days of the feast.[21]
- Death came to the houses that did not have the lamb's blood over the door at midnight.[22]
- The children of Israel had been commanded to pack and be ready to leave Egypt *before* the Passover feast.[95]

---

1 Exodus 12:21–24.

2 1 Corinthians 5:7.

3 Exodus 12:11, 27; Leviticus 23:5; Numbers 28:16.

4 Treseder, "Passover Promises Fulfilled in the Last Supper," April 1990 *Ensign*.

5 Boyd, *Days of Awe*, 47.

6 "Enrichment Section C: The Importance of Symbols," *Old Testament Student Manual*, 113.

7 Exodus 12:2.

8 Exodus 12:3.

9 Exodus 12:3–4.

10 Exodus 12:5.

11 Exodus 12:6.

12 Exodus 12:7, 13.

13 Exodus 12:8–9.

14 Exodus 12:46.

15 Exodus 12:8, 15–20, 34, 39.

16 Exodus 12:8.

17 Exodus 12:9–10.

18 Exodus 6:6–7, emphasis added.

19 Exodus 12:11.

20 Exodus 12:11, 27.

21 Exodus 12:16.

22 Exodus 12:29.

23 Exodus 11:2–3; 12:34–36.

CHAPTER 8

————— ❦ —————

The Messiah Born at Passover

But thou, Beth-lehem Ephratah,
though thou be little among the thousands of Judah,
yet out of thee shall he come forth unto me that is to be ruler in Israel;
whose goings forth have been from of old, from everlasting.[1]

President Gordon B. Hinckley once said, "There would be no Christmas if there had not been Easter."[2] Remarkably, what we celebrate at each of these events—the birth, atonement, death, and resurrection of the Savior—actually occurred at Passover.

Elder Bruce D. Porter, of the Seventy, said:

> An ancient Hebrew tradition held that the Messiah would be born at Passover. We know that that April in the meridian of time indeed fell in the week of the Passover feast—that sacred Jewish commemoration of Israel's salvation from the destroying angel that brought death to the firstborn sons of Egypt. Each Israelite family that sacrificed a lamb and smeared its blood on the wooden doorposts of their dwelling was spared (see Exodus 12:3–30). Thirty-three years after Christ's Passover birth, His blood was smeared on the wood posts of a cross to save His people from the destroying angels of death and sin.[3]

Some have wondered, on a practical level, why Mary and Joseph would have traveled to Bethlehem when they did, as Mary was so near to the time of her labor and delivery. Luke tells us that Caesar Augustus had decreed that "all the world should be taxed."[4] The "tax" referred to was actually a census from which taxes would be determined. Each head of a family was to register in the town of his ancestry, and thus, Joseph would register for the census in Bethlehem, the city of David.[5] It appears that Joseph timed his civic duties to align with the spiritual requirement to present himself at the temple for the Passover feast.

As discussed previously,[6] the population of Jerusalem and its environs swelled into the millions during the feast days. Bethlehem, only about six miles from Jerusalem, would have been crowded with pilgrims, who, like Joseph, combined their Passover responsibilities with their duties to the Roman government. It is not surprising then, that there was no room at the inn (or anywhere else) for Mary to find a private shelter. Families would be camped out everywhere throughout the land in a festive spirit of reunion and community. Did Mary and Joseph meet with relatives within the city or its outskirts? Was there another woman present to help Mary through her pains? We do not really know. What we *do* know is that the birth of Jesus would fulfill prophecies of promise to the very letter (or jot and tittle). In order to do so, there would be miraculous signs in the heavens, and special witnesses called to testify as they came to know that the Messiah had been born in Bethlehem, as long foretold.

Alfred Edersheim wrote:

> There is . . . testimony which seems to us not only reliable, but embodies most ancient Jewish tradition. It is contained in one of the smaller *Midrashim* . . . the so-called Messiah-Haggadah (*Aggadoth Mashiach*) opens as follows: "A star shall come out of Jacob. There is a Boraita in the name of the Rabbis: The heptad in which the Son of David cometh . . . and *the Star shall shine forth from the East and this is the Star of the Messiah.*"[7]

The first book of Genesis states that there should be "lights in the firmament of the heaven to divide the day from the night; and let them be for *signs*, and for seasons, and for days, and years."[8] A Passover evening is bright with the light of a full moon. If Jesus was born at Passover, His birth would have been flooded with light: the light of a full moon, the light of the great star, and the light of the "glory of the Lord." How fitting this light would be in heralding the birth of He who called Himself "The Light of the World."[9]

When we consider the sense of hopeful expectation that accompanied the Passover at the time of Jesus's birth, we might see the events as having more significance than we had previously understood. The angelic annunciation to the shepherds, for example, is better understood when we realize that the shepherds watching over the flock were likely priests who had responsibility for the flock designated for the temple.[10]

Alfred Edersheim explained that:

> There was near Bethlehem, on the road to Jerusalem, a tower known as *Migdal Eder*, or *the watchtower of the flock*. Here was the station where shepherds watched the flocks destined for the sacrifice in the temple . . . It was a settled conviction among the Jews that the Messiah was to be born in Bethlehem, and equally that he was to be revealed from Migdal Eder. The beautiful significance of the revelation of the infant Christ to shepherds watching the flocks destined for sacrifice needs no comment.[11]

The flock mentioned in the scripture, then, was apparently the one used for temple sacrifices, and the shepherds thus had responsibility for the most important flock in the region.

Gerald Lund explained:

> Sometimes in translation the power of the original language is considerably lessened. While the words, in English, of the angel to the shepherds are beautiful and significant, we miss much of the electrifying impact the original words must have had on those men of Judea . . . In essence, here is [the] pronouncement: "Unto you is born this day in the city prophesied to be the birthplace of the Messiah, *Yeshua* [or Jesus], the Savior, who is the Anointed One (the Messiah), and who is also Jehovah, the God of your fathers."[12]

Consider the weight of responsibility that lay upon the shepherds that night. It was springtime, and lambing season. The historian Josephus tells us that 250,000 lambs might be sacrificed for the Passover at that time.[13] It's hard to comprehend the numbers, and the earnest care the shepherds must take. They must watch the ewes carefully, not only to aid in the birthing process, but also, and most importantly, they must mark and separate the firstborn male, as it would be destined for the temple altars. These lambs must be inspected to make sure that they were perfect, without blemish, stain or crookedness. This was a sacred duty in which there could be no variance or turning aside. Yet, with the angelic announcement, certain shepherds *did* turn away from the ewes so that they might witness and testify that they had seen the birth of the Lamb of God, the Messiah for whom they had been waiting.[14]

---

1 Micah 5:2.

2 Hinckley, "The Wondrous and True Story of Christmas," Dec. 2000 *Ensign*.

3 Porter, "Come Let Us Adore Him," Dec. 2013 *Ensign*. See also Pratt, "Passover—Was it Symbolic of His Coming?" Jan. 1994 *Ensign*.

4 Luke 2:1.

5 See Luke 2:4.

6 See Chapter 1—Temple-Centered Holy Days.

7 Edersheim, *The Life and Times of Jesus the Messiah*, 147.

8 Genesis 1:14.

9 John 8:12.

10 Edersheim, *The Life and Times of Jesus the Messiah*, 131.

11 Ibid.

12 Lund, *Jesus Christ, Key to the Plan of Salvation,* 16–18.

13 Josephus, *War 6.9.3*, 422–27.

14 See Haymond, "Who Were the Shepherds in the the Christmas Story?" templestudy.com; Pack and Smith, "Who Were the Shepherds," redeemerofisrael.org; Wersen, "Keeping Watch: The Rabbinical Shepherds of Bethlehem," www.hisplacechurch.com.

CHAPTER 9

―――― ∽◯∾ ――――

Jesus at Passover, *Pesach*

And the . . . Passover was at hand . . .[1]

NOT ONLY WAS JESUS BORN AT PASSOVER, BUT HIS LIFE AND MIN-istry is marked by Passover events.

It was at Passover that Jesus, at twelve years of age, traveled with His parents and other family members to Jerusalem. While so little is recorded and known about Jesus's youth, this particular event stands out from the silence, and it is important for us to take notice.

It was customary, as we have previously discussed, for whole caravans comprised of friends and family to make the pilgrimage to Jerusalem for the feast days. After the festivities were over, Mary and Joseph had traveled a full day's journey towards home when they discovered that Jesus was not amongst the company. We can only imagine their concerns for His welfare, for they had a sacred commission to guard and keep Him safe. Harried and probably frantic after a three-day search, they found Jesus at the temple in the midst of "the doctors," or "teachers," holding discourse with them that "astonished" those professors with His wisdom and understanding.[2] Mary questioned Jesus, asking, "Son, why hast thou thus dealt with us? behold, thy father and I have sought thee sorrowing."[3] Jesus's response reveals the degree to which His self-awareness had matured:

"How is it that ye sought me? wist ye not that I must be about my Father's business?"[4]

James E. Talmage sheds some light on the incident:

> At twelve years of age a Jewish boy was recognized as a member of
> his home community; he was required then to enter with definite

41

purpose upon his chosen vocation; he attained an advanced status as an individual in that thereafter he could not be arbitrarily disposed of as a bond-servant by his parents; he was appointed to higher studies in school and home; and, when accepted by the priests, he became a "son of the law." It was the common and very natural desire of parents to have their sons attend the feast of the Passover and be present at the temple ceremonies as recognized members of the congregation when of the prescribed age.

Elder Talmage continues:

It was no unusual thing for a twelve year old boy to be questioned by priests, scribes, or rabbis, nor to be permitted to ask questions of these professional expounders of the law, for such procedure was part of the educational training of Jewish youths; nor was there anything surprising in such a meeting of students and teachers within the temple courts, for the rabbis of that time were accustomed to give instruction there; and people, young and old, gathered about them, sitting at their feet to learn; but there was much that was extraordinary in this interview as the demeanor of the learned doctors showed, for never before had such a student been found, inasmuch as "all that heard him were astonished at his understanding and answers."[5]

At thirty years of age, Jesus began His public ministry in Jerusalem at Passover, as recorded by John.[6] This was the first time He cleansed the temple, declaring "Take these things hence; make not my Father's house an house of merchandise."[7] This public declaration of His Parentage, and His protective zeal for the temple, instigated the enmity that the High Priest(s) felt for Him throughout His ministry.

In terms of Passover symbolism, it is notable that Jesus took upon Himself the role of cleansing the temple and declaring it His Father's house, because it was the duty of the father of each household to make a show of searching the home for leaven that must be removed before the Passover could be celebrated. This ritual became a time of delight and playfulness for the family, as the mother would have already scrubbed the home from top to bottom, and had alerted the father as to where crumbs of leaven could be found for the purpose of his hunt. He would have a feather in one hand, and a wooden spoon in the other, in which he would gather those stray crumbs, wrap them up, and take them outside to be burned in a communal fire.

Jesus's cleansing of the temple was not in fun, however, and illustrated the serious concern that Israel's households must be rid of any corruption, represented by the leaven. If the temple were unclean, and the restrictions for its use had been taken lightly, how could the individual family households be expected to understand the importance of cleansing their own homes of sin, as well as the inner vessel?

The great Bread of Life sermon was given at Passover.[8] Bread, or specifically, unleavened bread, is a central part of the Passover celebration. The Feast of Unleavened Bread began officially the day after Passover, but was combined with the Passover feast from earliest time. As discussed previously, all leaven was to be removed from the house before the Passover could begin. Leaven, or yeast, as we know it, represents corruption, pride, or any substance that can spoil purity. The Israelites carried unleavened bread with them out of Egypt and into the wilderness. It had to sustain them for a long time without becoming unfit for consumption, but perhaps it also symbolized the need to leave the corrupting influences of Egypt behind them.

The unleavened bread used today, the *matzah*, is produced under strict guidelines. It is pierced, so that it does not rise or bubble up in baking, it is pressed flat, and "beaten," so that there appear to be stripes or "bruises" on the bread. *Jesus was also beaten, pressed in the "Olive Press" of the Garden in Gethsemane, bruised, and pierced.*

Although we do not know that it was *unleavened* bread that Jesus and His followers partook of at the Bread of Life sermon, John tells us that the "Passover was nigh,"[9] and certainly bread was on their minds, as Jesus performed the miracle of feeding 5,000 from a few loaves and two fishes.[10] In fact, Jesus accused the people of following Him simply because they wanted more bread to eat.[11]

In the discussion that followed Jesus's assessment of their desires, He told the people:

> *I am the bread of life:*
> *he that cometh to me shall never hunger;*
> *and he that believeth on me shall never thirst . . .*
> *I am the living bread which came down from heaven:*
> *if any man eat of this bread, he shall live for ever:*

and the bread that I will give is my flesh,
which I will give for the life of the world . . .
Verily, verily I say unto you,
Except ye eat the flesh of the Son of man,
and drink his blood, ye have no life in you.
Whoso eateth my flesh, and drinketh my blood, hath eternal life;
and I will raise him up at the last day.
For my flesh is meat indeed, and my blood is drink indeed.
He that eateth my flesh, and drinketh my blood,
dwelleth in me, and I in him.[12]

It was this sermon, about eating His flesh and drinking His blood that offended many of His own disciples, who felt they could no longer follow Him.[13] Yet, it was at another Passover—and His last—that Jesus instituted the sacrament, to be partaken of in remembrance of His flesh and blood given in our behalf that we might be redeemed, and have eternal life.

One particularly poignant aspect of the Feast occurs when, at the Passover dinner, three matzahs are displayed to the congregation. The middle one is taken, broken, and one piece is placed between the other two whole pieces, while the remaining broken piece is wrapped in a white cloth and "hidden" somewhere in the room for the children to find later. Once it is found, this piece is distributed and shared amongst the diners. It is called the *Afikomen*, the "dessert" or last taste of the evening, which is considered "sweeter than sweet," and is meant to linger on the tongue. Many believe that Jesus used the Afikomen for the first sacramental instruction.

This ritual of the three pieces of matzah bread, with the middle piece broken, and one part of that hidden, has caused a great deal of discussion over the years. What could it mean? Chabad.org, a Jewish site dedicated to the feasts and festivals explains that "the piece that remains on the Seder Plate is the 'poor man's bread' over which the tale of our slavery is said. Poor people only eat a small part of their bread—they need to save the rest in case tomorrow there is none."[14]

Rabbi Harold Schulweis wrote the following about the broken and hidden matzah:

Brokenness is a symbol of incompletion. Life is not whole. The Passover itself is not complete. The Passover we celebrate deals with the past redemption of our people from bondage in Egypt. That redemption is a fact of history and it heartens us because through its recollection we know that our hope for a future redemption is not fantasy. . . .

But it is toward the Passover of the Future that our memories are directed. The *redemption is not over.* There is fear and poverty and sickness. There is trembling on earth. . . . The broken matzah speaks to our times, shakes us by the shoulders and shouts into our hearts, "Do not bury your spirit in history. Do not think it is over, complete, that the Messiah has come and you have nothing to do but to wait, to pray, to believe."

The history of our liberation is not for the sake of gloating over the past but for confirmation of our hopes. Even as we retrieve the past, the future is held before us. We begin the story of our past affliction with an appeal for present help and with an eye set upon the future . . .

The hidden matzah is the greater part. The promise of the future is greater than the achievements of the past. It is no game to keep the child awake, this secret. It is the vision of messianic times toward which we live and struggle.[15]

There are hundreds of interpretations for the broken and hidden matzah, but Rabbi Schulweis's resonates with a yearning for a messianic fulfillment.

We might consider that the three pieces of unleavened bread point to the three members of the Godhead, with Christ the broken piece in the center. As with those who heard the Bread of Life sermon, many don't recognize Jesus as the Messiah and Redeemer, or realize how desperately they need Him. His reality may be "hidden" from our view. We must humble ourselves, and "become like a little child" to find Him.[16] Once Christ is discovered and we partake of His Atonement, our life can become sweet and full.

One author offers an additional insight into the broken middle piece. He writes:

I am taking this second whole piece and breaking a portion from it to represent the Messiah, which is put away to return at the end of the meal, thus symbolizing that the redemption through Messiah would take place in two phases, the second at a later time.

The same author adds:

After the destruction of the temple Judaism incorporated the early messianic tradition of the Afikomen to be a substitute for the lamb in the ceremony which was the final food of the Seder feast. However they did not identify with it as the buried and risen Messiah. The Afikomen is a symbolic type of the death and resurrection of Yeshua where the bread of affliction is wrapped in grave clothes as it were, to come forth at the end of the feast as the resurrected body of the Messiah.[17]

Each symbol offers an opportunity to see many layers of meaning. It also offers us the chance to join together as a community of those who love God. Whether we are on the level of the children who are joyfully hunting the Afikomen, following Rabbi Schulweis in his yearning for redemption through the Messiah, or pondering the idea that the broken matzah might possibly point to two appearances of the Messiah, the Passover gives us the opportunity for discussion, and through that discussion, a binding together of hearts in hopeful faith. Passover has been called "a talk feast," and it certainly can be that, if we allow the time for reflection and the Spirit to guide.

As we consider the heartfelt thoughts that have been shared in this chapter by a practicing rabbi, a Messianic Jew, and a secular Jew, may we remember Nephi's charge to "remember the Jews," and seek to love and recover them.[18] Only in a spirit of gratitude, compassion, and love, as well as an acknowledgement of what they have preserved for us in the scriptures and in faith practices, will we ever be able to share the glad tidings they are yearning to hear.

Finally, as we reflect upon Jesus, and Passover events He participated in, we ponder the fact that He died at Passover in fulfillment of all that Passover had symbolized for thousands of years. He went as a "lamb to the slaughter," and "poured out his soul unto death: . . . [in order to] bare the sin of many."[19]

1 John 2:13.
2 Luke 2:42–47.
3 Luke 2:48.
4 Luke 2:49.
5 Talmage, *Jesus the Christ,* 107–8.
6 John 2:13–25.
7 John 2:15–16.
8 See John 6:4.
9 John 6:4.
10 John 6:5–13.
11 John 6:26.
12 John 6:35, 51, 53–56.
13 John 6:66–125.
14 "Yachatz—Break the Middle Matzah," chabad.org.
15 Schulweis, "The Hidden Matzah," https://www.myjewishlearning.com.
16 Matthew 18:3; Mosiah 3:19.
17 Hebrew Roots, "The Haggadah: 'The Telling of the Passover Story'" https://zims-en.kiwix. campusafrica.gos.orange.com/wikibooks_en_all_maxi/A/Hebrew_Roots/Holy_Days/ Passover/Service.
18 2 Nephi 29:5.
19 Isaiah 53:7, 12.

—— ∾⊚⊱ ——

CHAPTER 10

Jesus Christ: Lamb of God and Messiah

The Lamb slain from the foundation of the world[1]

THE PASSOVER LAMB WAS TO BE SELECTED ON THE 10TH OF NISAN and put to death on the 14th. Under the rule of the High Priests Annas and Caiaphas at the time of Jesus's ministry, offerers hesitated to bring their own lamb as an offering, for fear that it would be ruled unfit during inspection so that they were forced to purchase from the temple market. This corruption incensed Jesus, and caused Him to accuse the High Priests of making His Father's House a house of merchandise.[2]

In simpler times, a family would select a perfect firstborn male lamb from amongst their flocks and bring it into their home on the 10th day. By the time the 14th arrived, with its appointed time for slaughter, everyone would have fallen in love with the lamb, and the sacrifice would be particularly difficult to make.

It is sobering to realize that the day that all Jerusalem seemed to proclaim their love for Jesus as their Messiah was the 10th of Nisan. That day is referred to by historians as the "triumphal entry," when Jesus rode into Jerusalem on a donkey, and people waved palm branches, spread their clothes before Him, and shouted "Hosanna! Blessed is the King of Israel that cometh in the name of the Lord!"[3] "Hosanna to the Son of David!"[4]

Jesus made His way directly to the temple, and cleansed it the second time, this time proclaiming that it was *His* house.[5] The Lamb was "in the house," and the people knew and loved Him, but the priests who were threatened by His power over the people, determined that He should die—and that He would be put to death on the 14th, as foreshadowed by the Passover sacrifice.[6]

"My time is at hand," Jesus explained to His apostles, as He gave them instructions to go and make ready a place for them to partake of the Passover meal together. ". . . The Son of Man is betrayed to be crucified," He added.[7] Jesus and His apostles partook of their meal in a somber mood that night, in contrast to the many other pilgrims who would participate in an attitude of light-hearted celebration.

Judas, full of guilt, had already made his arrangements with the high priests to betray Jesus to their guards. "We mark the deep symbolic significance of it all, in that the Lord was, so to speak, paid for out of the Temple-money which was destined for the purchase of sacrifices, and that He, Who took on Him the form of a servant, was sold and bought at the legal price of a slave."[8]

Jesus and His disciples kept the Passover on the first day of the feast.[9] Don't let the Jewish method of time-keeping confuse you: they marked it as one day—sundown to sundown (for example, a Thursday after sundown to Friday at sundown, or some believe it was actually a Wednesday and Thursday). The poorer folk would celebrate the first day, while the priests and other wealthy citizens would partake of the Passover meal the second day. The priests had the duty to sacrifice approximately 250,000 lambs for Passover, and would sacrifice for their own table last of all. These last sacrifices were offered at 2:30 in the afternoon.

Luke states that the Savior sent Peter and John to make provisions for the Passover.[10] How fitting it seems that these two would enter temple grounds with the lamb for sacrifice, and witness all of the proceedings. They would also be called upon to witness the proceedings of the sacrifice of the true Lamb, and they were the first apostles to witness the empty grave.

In the temple courtyard, a company of priests stood in two lines, holding golden and silver bowls. As a lamb was slain, a priest would fill the bowl with its blood, then pass the bowl up the line until the priest nearest the altar would take it and throw the blood in one jet at the base of the altar. All the while this was transpiring, a solemn hymn of praise was raised, the "Hallel," comprised from Psalm 113–118. Included in the Hallel are the phrases: "Save now, I beseech thee, O Lord: O Lord, I beseech thee, send now prosperity. Blessed be he that cometh in the name of the Lord."[11]

The Passover feast has a specific form; every Jewish family would be saying the same prayers and eating the same food. The foods were deeply symbolic, and were eaten in a particular order. There were four "cups" of wine taken throughout the meal, and unleavened bread was eaten at various intervals. The Passover ritual is a beautiful expression of remembrance, thanksgiving, dedication and hope. There are many passages that are particularly poignant as they pertain to the circumstances of the night of the Lord's "Last Supper." We will attempt to review the proceedings as they have been ordered throughout the years, and relate their occurrence either to the actual evening with the Lord, or to their fulfillment in His life, ministry and Atonement.

The Passover begins with ritualistic lighting of candles, with the woman of the house reciting the phrase: "The Lord bless thee, and keep thee, the Lord make his face shine upon thee, and be gracious unto thee: the Lord lift up his countenance upon thee, and give thee peace."[12] This prayer also corresponded to the daily prayer offered with the burning of incense at the temple at 3:00, for *the hour of prayer*. The constant prayer of Israel was to behold the face of the Messiah. *Was not this very prayer fulfilled in the ministry of Jesus of Nazareth?*

The first cup of wine is raised by the head of the table, in this case Jesus. The name of the cup is "**I Will Bring You Out**." This cup celebrates the promise of Jehovah to bring His people out of Egypt. Jesus invites His followers to come out of a spiritual wasteland, and into the Kingdom of God, where they will be equal heirs with Him. This cup can be related to the first step in the ancient temple, where priests, as proxies, symbolically acted out a reversal of the Fall, suggesting that mankind could make their way out of (and away from) the world, and back into the presence of the Father. The first step was symbolized by the altar of sacrifice in the outer courtyard, and visible to all onlookers. The altar was symbolically located "in the world" or the telestial kingdom. Even as the first Passover cup represented the invitation to come out of Egypt, obedience to God in offering up a sacrifice represented the desire to align one's life with the will of God, and to sacrifice anything that stood in the way of an ultimate union with Him, whether that be a prized possession, a cherished habit, or a favorite sin.

Many people looked for their Messiah to be a military-type hero who would lead their forces, or at least deliver them with the same mighty miracles as shown at the time of deliverance from Egypt. However, Jesus's deliverance from sin comes through His meekness and humility, His complete submission to the will of the Father in performing the Atonement in our behalf. He modeled what was necessary for our own path to salvation, represented by the altar of sacrifice: submission of our own will. Elder Neal A. Maxwell explained that "the submission of one's will is really the only uniquely personal thing we have to place on God's altar."[13]

Following the presentation of the first Passover cup, all present wash their hands. Many believe that it was at this point, early in the evening, that Jesus girded Himself as a servant and washed the feet of the disciples. John indicates that Jesus also washed Judas's feet. What were the thoughts of Jesus and Judas during this ministration? Jesus pronounced afterwards: "Ye are clean, but not all. For he knew who should betray him."[14] Yet, nevertheless, He lovingly performed the service, leading by His example.

Karpas, or a fresh herb like parsley, is dipped in saltwater, representing the fruitfulness of hope that God remembers His people. The saltwater represents their tears. We think of the promise: "For the Lamb which is in the midst of the throne shall feed them, and shall lead them unto living fountains of waters: and God shall wipe away all tears from their eyes."[15]

The unleavened bread is shown to those present. The middle matzah is broken, and one piece is hidden to be found by the children, and savored as the *Affikomen* later in the meal. The bread is now broken, blessed, and distributed.

At one point in the feast, the youngest son, or the youngest man present (probably John at the Last Supper), would ask: "Wherefore is this night distinguished from all other nights?" In other words, "What makes this night different from other nights?" It's sobering to consider that question being asked at Jesus's table (if it was). What distinguished *that* Passover from all other Passovers? It was *the* night, *the* Passover, upon which the salvation of all mankind would rely; it surpasses all other nights in its significance.

Bitter herbs are eaten to symbolize the bitterness of bondage and slavery under the Egyptians. How much more bitter is the bondage of sin!

The second cup, named "**I Will Deliver You,**" is raised, blessed and drunk. The blessing on the cup is: "Blessed art thou, Jehovah, our God, King of the Universe, who hast redeemed us. We give thanks to Thee for our deliverance and for the redemption of our souls. Blessed art thou, O Jehovah, who hast redeemed Israel." The Atonement of Jesus Christ, Jehovah, delivers "prisoners" on both sides of the veil.

The Second Cup corresponds to the second step within the ancient temple ritual, and the journey back to God: the menorah, located on the left-hand side within the holy place. The menorah represents the tree of life, which Nephi came to understand as representing the "love of God," and the Atonement of the Savior.[16] The light of the menorah also represented the light of God's word, or the Gospel, shining out from the temple to all the world. That light was to be kept forever burning as a promise of deliverance from sin and death through the light of Christ, and His gracious Atonement in our behalf.

As the Seder progresses, the participants join in a recitation cataloging the miracles surrounding Israel's deliverance. All present exclaim: *"By the blood of the lamb was Israel spared. By the blood of the lamb was Jacob redeemed. By the blood of the lamb was death made to pass over."*

At Jesus's table, at some point earlier in the evening, a dispute had arisen over which of the apostles should be "accounted the greatest."[17] Elder Bruce R. McConkie believed the dispute may have been over the seating arrangement for the evening:

> By instinct we feel Judas—who was out of harmony with his brethren—was at the root of the trouble. With whom would he contend? Obviously with Peter, who was in fact the chief apostle and who knew his place was at the Lord's side . . . when Jesus rebuked the contention, a very natural thing would happen: impetuous Peter would go and take the lowest seat, while spiritually hardened Judas,

immune to feelings of conscience and decency, would maintain his claim and take the seat of honor at the side of Jesus.[18]

Elder McConkie's theory is substantiated by the fact that Peter was the first to be washed by the Lord, being at the end or foot of the "U" shaped table, and Judas received the sop from the Savior's own hand.[19] The "sop" was a kind of sandwich made from the bread, herbs and lamb.

The giving of the sop was a mark of affection, and the fact that Judas would accept it knowing full well his intention of betrayal is yet another sign of his hardness of heart. The Savior had said: "One of you shall betray me."[20] All of the disciples were deeply troubled by His announcement, and each of them inquired: "Is it I?"[21] Jesus told John and Peter that the person to whom He gave the sop was the traitor. As He gave the morsel to Judas, He told him: "That thou doest, do quickly."[22] Once Judas departed, the mood in the room lightened considerably.

Some think that it may have been the hidden *Afikomen* that Jesus took and provided with new symbolism as He used it to initiate the first sacrament. That sweet dessert, emblematic of so many of the characteristics of the Savior, would fit the need beautifully. The ritual search for the *Afikomen* reminds us of His promises: "And ye shall seek me, and find me, when ye shall search for me with all of your heart," and "Draw near unto me and I will draw near unto you; seek me diligently and ye shall find me; ask, and ye shall receive, knock, and it shall be opened unto you."[23]

> *And as they did eat, Jesus took bread and blessed it, and*
> *brake, and gave to them and said, Take it, and eat.*
> *Behold this is for you to do in remembrance of my body;*
> *for as oft as ye do this ye will remember this hour that I was with you.*[24]

Everyone seems to agree that it was the third cup, called "**I Will Redeem You**," that the Savior used to institute the sacrament of His blood. There is a lengthy recitation accompanying its presentation, including a moment where all participants join in one voice in exclaiming: "May He who is most merciful, make us worthy to behold the day of the Messiah!" Imagine the hearts of the disciples, remembering this earnest plea from past Passover celebrations, and seeing now the face of the Messiah, and knowing that He was soon to die!

> *And he took the cup, and when he had given thanks,*
> *he gave it to them; and they all drank of it.*
> *And he said unto them,*
> *This is in remembrance of my blood which is shed for many*
> *and the new testament which I give unto you;*
> *for of me ye shall bear record unto all the world.*
> *And as oft as ye do this ordinance,*
> *ye will remember me in this hour that I was with you*
> *and drank with you of this cup,*
> *even the last time in my ministry.*
> *And now they were grieved, and wept over him.*[25]

Following our earlier endeavor to relate the Passover cups to the progressive journey of the priests in the ancient temple, we consider the third step in that journey: the table of shewbread.

The table of shewbread, referred to in Hebrew as "the bread of faces," or "the bread of the presence,"[26] held twelve loaves of bread weighing approximately ten pounds each. Matthew B. Brown notes that pitchers and cups of pure gold were also set on the table, and were likely used for distributing and consuming wine along with the bread every Sabbath day.[27] The symbolic relationship to the sacrament of the Lord's table is inescapable. For the Israelites, they may have been reminded of the fact that seventy elders of Israel accepted the invitation to meet the Lord on Sinai, and to eat and drink with Him,[28] entering into a covenant relationship by doing so.

Each Passover cup is to be completely drained; it is not to be sipped, or set aside. And so it is with our entering into a covenant with the Savior for redemption through His Atonement. We are *all in*, as symbolized by our immersion at baptism, or we are like those who remained at the foot of Mt. Sinai, *meaning* to commit, perhaps even *wanting* to commit, yet still holding back.

Jesus did not hold back. Although the cup He drank was more awful than He had supposed,[29] He would "not shrink" from it.[30] He drained it to its bitter dregs, and brought the promise of life and salvation to His people.[31]

The feast closes with the drinking of the fourth cup, called "**I Will Take You To Me**." Most believe that Jesus and His apostles did not partake of the fourth cup. Matthew records that after partaking of the Cup of Redemption (the Third Cup) wherein He instituted the sacrament, Jesus said, "I will not drink henceforth of this fruit of the vine, until the day when I drink it new with you in my Father's kingdom."[32] It is moving and beautiful to note that almost at this very point in the ceremony as it would typically have been followed, Jesus promised His disciples:

Let not your heart be troubled:
ye believe in God, believe also in me.
In my Father's house are many mansions:
if it were not so, I would have told you.
I go to prepare a place for you.
And if I go and prepare a place for you, I will come again,
and receive you unto myself;
that where I am, there ye may be also.[33]

Jesus goes to prepare a place for us, and when those preparations are complete, He will "take us to Him," and to the Father. The fourth step in the ancient temple was the altar of incense, which stood before the veil, and represented the prayers of the saints. The "innermost part of the worship of the day" took place at the hour of prayer at 3:00 each day. The officiating priest would put fresh incense on the altar, and offer a ritual prayer, as the people prostrated themselves in the outer courtyard, joining their hearts in one unified plea. Their prayer was hope for deliverance, the blessings of peace, and above all, that they might behold the face of the Lord, and enter within the veil and into His presence.[34]

The Passover symbols and images testify of Jesus Christ in all of their details. Imagine going through all the motions of repeating these beautifully deep and symbolic rituals, and missing Him! Other families were partaking of the same Passover emblems that holy night of Gethsemane and the next day of Calvary. These included people who had seen the Messiah's face, but rejected Him. Others had walked by, giving Him little thought in their lives. We can make the same grievous error when we partake of the emblems of the sacrament without thinking. When we do so, we are in danger of taking the Lord's name in vain—meaning partaking in His name, but without really using the gift He offers.

The drinking of each Passover cup was associated with a promise of coming nearer to Christ in a progressive step-by-step journey, even as the furnishings of the ancient temple represented a step-by-step return to the presence of God in the Holy of Holies.

Christ promises deliverance and redemption, but the participant's drinking of the cup fully, even as we fully drink of the sacrament cup today, represented an "all-in" commitment on their part as well. Eating the bread or drinking the water represents our own personal commitment to accept and partake of what Jesus offers: we have to be *willing* to leave Egypt or Babylon in order for Him to bring us out of darkness. We show that willingness through our obedience to His commandments, and the sacrifice of any temptation or influence that is keeping us from Him. He can deliver and redeem us only as we are *willing* to change our minds and our behavior, to repent of our sins, live by His gospel, and put our trust in Him. He can take us into the Father's kingdom and presence only as we are *willing* to yoke ourselves with Him, and consecrate our lives to His work, and honor our covenants with Him.

Elder Jeffrey R. Holland remarked:

Since that upper room experience on the eve of Gethsemane and Golgotha, children of the promise have been under covenant to remember Christ's sacrifice in this newer, higher, more holy and personal way. . . .

If remembering is the principal task before us, what might come to our memory when those plain and precious emblems are offered to us?

. . . [E]very ordinance of the gospel focuses in one way or another on the atonement of the Lord Jesus Christ, and surely that is why this particular ordinance with all its symbolism and imagery comes to us more readily and more repeatedly than any other in our life. It comes in what has been called "the most sacred, the most holy, of all the meetings of the Church."[35]

Perhaps we do not always attach that kind of meaning to our weekly sacramental service. How "sacred" and how "holy" is it? Do we see it as our passover, remembrance of *our* safety and deliverance and redemption?

With so much at stake, this ordinance commemorating our escape from the angel of darkness should be taken more seriously than it sometimes is. It should be a powerful, reverent, reflective moment. It should encourage spiritual feelings and impressions. As such it should not be rushed. It is not something to "get over" so that the real purpose of a sacrament meeting can be pursued. This *is* the real purpose of the meeting. And everything that is said or sung or prayed in those services should be consistent with the grandeur of this sacred ordinance.

. . . One request Christ made of his disciples on that night of deep anguish and grief was that they stand by him, stay with him in his hour of sorrow and pain. "Could ye not watch with me one hour?" he asked longingly.[36] I think he asks that again of us, every Sabbath day when the emblems of his life are broken and blessed and passed.[37]

---

1 Revelation 13:8.
2 John 2:16.
3 John 12:12–13.
4 Matthew 21:9.
5 Matthew 21:12–13; Luke 19:46.
6 John 11:50–53.
7 Matthew 26:2, 18.
8 Edersheim, *The Life and Times of Jesus the Messiah*, 803; Matt. 26:14–16, 27:6.
9 Mark 14:12.
10 Luke 22:8.
11 Edersheim, *The Temple: It's Ministry and Services*, 175–76; Psalm 118:25–26.
12 Numbers 6:24–26.
13 Maxwell, "Swallowed Up in the Will of the Father," October 1995 General Conference.
14 John 13:4–11.
15 Revelation 7:17.
16 1 Nephi 11:8–23.
17 Luke 22:24.
18 McConkie, *The Mortal Messiah*, 4:31–32.
19 John 13:5–6, 26.
20 John 13:21.
21 Matthew 26:22.

22 John 13:27.

23 Jeremiah 29:13; Doctrine and Covenants 88:63.

24 Joseph Smith Translation, Mark 14:20–21.

25 Joesph Smith Translation, Mark 14:22–26.

26 Wilson, *Wilson's Old Testament Word Studies*, s.v. "shew, shew-bread," 388.

27 Brown, *The Gate of Heaven*, 70.

28 Exodus 24:9–11.

29 Matthew 26:39.

30 Doctrine and Covenants 19:18.

31 See Cherry, *Redemption of the Bride: God's Redeeming Love for His Covenant People*, Chapter 2.

32 Matthew 26:29.

33 John 14:1–3.

34 See Edersheim, *The Temple: Its Ministry and Services*, 128–29.

35 Smith, *Doctrines of Salvation*, 2:340.

36 Matthew 26:40

37 Holland, "'This Do in Remembrance of Me," Oct. 1995 General Conference.

CHAPTER 11

A Cup for Elijah

Each of the cups of Passover hold special significance, including a cup set aside for Elijah the prophet. The last prophecy of the Old Testament records a promise that Elijah would come again, and precede the coming of the Messiah:

Behold, I will send you Elijah the prophet
before the coming of the great and dreadful day of the
Lord: And he shall turn the hearts of the
fathers to the children, and the heart of the children to their fathers,
lest I come and smite the earth with a curse.[1]

Because it was the last accepted prophecy, this promise holds great weight for the Jewish people. During a portion of the Passover seder, the door is opened, and the participants chant:

Elijah the Prophet, Elijah the Tishbite,
Elijah, Elijah, Elijah the Gileadite!
May he come, soon in our day,
Ushering in the Messiah—son of David!

It's important to recognize that while the current Passover Seder, or Haggadah, commemorates Israel's deliverance from bondage, it also looks forward to a future deliverance, as evidenced by the cup for Elijah, who would usher in a new Messianic age.

Elijah ministered amongst the ten tribes in the Northern Kingdom of Israel, who had become apostate. His contest with the priests of Baal drew a lot of attention, but very few converts.[2] Elijah was so discouraged that he felt completely alone in his faith, and asked the Lord to take his life.[3] He had had an extremely difficult mission, and longed for release. The Lord knew and loved Elijah, however, and reassured him that his mission had not been in vain. As a final sign of favor, Elijah was taken into heaven in a chariot of fire, and did not taste of death.[4]

It is with joyful thanksgiving that we can report that in fulfillment of prophecy, Elijah *did* come to usher in the Messiah as part of the latter-day Restoration, *and he came on Passover,* just as anticipated. Elijah came to the Kirtland Temple April 3, 1836, to restore the sealing keys of the priesthood—turning the hearts of the children to the fathers, and to the promises of the covenant.[5]

The Doctrine and Covenants clarifies: "Behold, I will reveal unto you the Priesthood, by the hand of Elijah the prophet, before the coming of the great and dreadful day of the Lord. And he shall plant in the hearts of the children the promises made to the fathers, and the hearts of the children shall turn to their fathers. If it were not so, the whole earth would be utterly wasted at his coming."[6]

One of Elijah's roles in the Restoration was to "plant in the hearts of the children the promises made to the fathers," including promises that are foreshadowed in the ancient feast and festival days. It is of note that the interest in the ancient holy days has been renewed in our generation, and the study of them is bringing people to the Messiah, Jesus Christ. Perhaps this is an additional manifestation of the "Spirit of Elijah," that we typically associate with the worldwide interest in family history work.

But more, Elijah specifically restored the sealing keys, enabling families to be sealed together for eternity. These keys seem to be especially significant for Passover, as it celebrates God's deliverance and redemption of His people, and not just as a past event.

In His hometown of Nazareth, Jesus stood to take a turn at reading from the Sabbath text in His local synagogue. The reading for each sabbath was pre-determined, and on this day, the text was from Isaiah, and prophesied of the role of the promised Messiah:

> *The Spirit of the Lord God is upon me;*
> *because the Lord hath anointed me*
> *to preach good tidings unto the meek;*
> *he hath sent me to bind up the brokenhearted,*
> *to proclaim liberty to the captives,*
> *and the opening of the prison to them that are bound;*

To proclaim the acceptable year of the Lord,
and the day of vengeance of our God;
to comfort all that mourn;
To appoint unto them that mourn in Zion,
to give unto them beauty for ashes,
the oil of joy for mourning,
the garment of praise for the spirit of heaviness;
that they might be called the trees of righteousness,
the planting of the Lord,
that he might be glorified.
And they shall build the old wastes,
they shall raise up the former desolations,
and they shall repair the waste cities,
the desolations of many generations.[7]

When Jesus finished the reading, He testified: "This day is this scripture fulfilled in your ears."[8]

Jesus's binding up the brokenhearted, His proclamation of liberty to the captives, and the opening of the prison for those that are bound was fulfilled temporally in the actual story of the exodus of the children of Israel, but it is also fulfilled anew in our day. The promises made to the fathers can now see fruition because of the restoration of the priesthood and the priesthood keys. Those promises most often were centered on hope for the generations that would follow—hope that they might be enfolded in the covenant family, that they might know the joy of the gospel, and be one in the peace of the Lord. As we have discovered, that loving intent goes both directions: the parents to those who come after, and the children to those who went before. Those who have mourned the death of loved ones may now rejoice that the gift of resurrection is real because of the Atonement of Christ, and the sealing keys restored through Elijah can bind families together forever.

O death, where is thy sting?
O grave, where is thy victory?
. . . Thanks be to God, which giveth us the victory
through our Lord Jesus Christ.[9]

Malachi recorded yet another prophecy of hope:

Behold, I will send my messenger,
and he shall prepare the way before me:
and the Lord whom ye seek, shall suddenly come to his temple,
even the messenger of the covenant, whom ye delight in:
behold, he shall come, saith the Lord of hosts.[10]

As with almost all prophecies, and particularly those of the Old Testament, this promise has many layers of fulfillment. But, if we link it to the previous Malachi prophecy about Elijah who was to come before the great and dreadful day of the Lord, we might see one fulfillment as taking place on that beautiful Passover day at the Kirtland Temple when the Lord *did* come suddenly to His temple. And Elijah came too, saying:

Therefore, the keys of this dispensation
are committed into your hands;
and by this ye may know
that the great and dreadful day of the Lord is near,
even at the doors.[11]

He is coming! The Lord, in whom we delight, and for whom we seek, is coming soon—"even at the doors!"

The yearning for the Messiah echoes throughout the ages. Yet, tragically, He was "wounded in the house of [His] friends."[12] *Are we also in danger of missing that which we yearn for most?*

---

1 Malachi 4:5–6.
2 See 1 Kings 18:21–38.
3 1 Kings 19:4, 14.
4 2 Kings 2:11.
5 Doctrine and Covenants 110:13–16.
6 Doctrine and Covenants 2:1–3.
7 Isaiah 61:1–4.
8 Luke 4:21.
9 1 Corinthians 15:55–57.
10 Malachi 3:1.
11 Doctrine and Covenants 110:16.
12 Zechariah 13:6.

CHAPTER 12

—⁓◎⁓—

The Night of Watchings

After the Passover meal, Jesus and His Apostles made their way to the Garden of Gethsemane, where, with numerous other pilgrims, they would keep "The Night of Watchings." Over the years, the Israelites came to interpret the instructions in Exodus 12:42 to "observe the night" of Passover as a duty to stay awake all night keeping vigil, and "watching" for the Lord to deliver them.[1]

As they walked towards the Mount of Olives, Jesus and the Apostles were weighed down with sorrow and dread. In fact, Mark writes that "the disciples began to be sore amazed, and to be very heavy, and to complain in their hearts, wondering if this be the Messiah."[2] We can only imagine the burden this added to the Savior, when even His beloved friends began to doubt Him. He instructed the disciples to sit, watch, and pray, while He took Peter, James, and John as witnesses with Him to the place where He would begin His "preparations unto the children of men."[3] He told them: "My soul is exceeding sorrowful, even unto death: tarry ye here, and watch with me."[4]

The Apostles were weak that night; unable to even "watch one hour," they slept because of their overwhelming sadness.[5] "They said unto him, "The spirit truly is ready, but the flesh is weak."[6] They *wanted* to fulfill their mission, but they were overcome by their human frailties. Jesus faced the horror of the night without the aid of any mortal to offer comfort. He sweat blood for those who unwittingly slept a "stone's throw away," as well as for Judas and the priests who were plotting together even as He offered Himself in their behalf.

Now . . . when Jesus knew that his hour was come
that he should depart out of this world unto the Father,

having loved his own which were in the world,
he loved them unto the end.[7]

Jesus had taught, "Greater love hath no man than this, that a man lay down his life for his friends,"[8] and this He had determined to do before the foundations of this world were laid.[9] He was "the Lamb slain from the foundation of the world."[10] Love motivated Him, and love sustained Him through the lonely night and the torturous day that followed. It's almost impossible to conceive of such a love, that despite the suffering endured for each one of us—and even *because* of us—He could see, know, and love us so completely.

And he went a little further, and fell on his face,
and prayed, saying, O my Father, if it be possible,
let this cup pass from me:
nevertheless not as I will, but as thou wilt.
And there appeared an angel unto him from heaven,
strengthening him.
And being in an agony he prayed more earnestly:
and he sweat as it were
great drops of blood falling down to the ground.[11]

Elder James E. Talmage wrote:

Christ's agony in the Garden in unfathomable by the finite mind, both as to intensity and cause. . . . He struggled and groaned under a burden such as no other being who has lived on earth might even conceive as possible. It was not physical pain, nor mental anguish alone, that caused him to suffer such torture as to produce an extrusion of blood from every pore; but a spiritual agony of soul such as only God was capable of experiencing. . . . In that hour of anguish Christ met and overcame all the horrors that Satan, "the prince of this world," could inflict. . . . In some manner, actual and terribly real though to man incomprehensible, the Savior took upon Himself the burden of the sins of mankind from Adam to the end of the world."[12]

The Savior, Himself, expressed it thusly:

. . . Which suffering caused myself, even God,
the greatest of all,
to tremble because of pain,
and to bleed at every pore,
and to suffer both body and spirit—
and would that I might not drink the bitter cup, and shrink—
Nevertheless, glory be to the Father,
and I partook
and finished my preparations unto the children of men.[13]

Note the emphasis in the Doctrine and Covenants verse is not on avoiding the cup, but on not *shrinking* when partaking of it. Elder Neal A. Maxwell explained:

Several scriptures describe the essence of that glorious and rescuing Atonement, including a breathtaking, autobiographical verse confiding how Jesus "would that I might not drink the bitter cup, and shrink." Since the "infinite atonement" required infinite suffering, the risk of recoil was there![14] All humanity hung on the hinge of Christ's character! Mercifully, He did not shrink but "finished [His] preparations unto the children of men."[15]

On another occasion, Elder Maxwell explained:

. . . Christ confides in us His chief anxiety, namely, that He "would that [He] might not drink the bitter cup, and shrink"—especially desiring not to get partway through the Atonement and then pull back.[16]

With so much emphasis on "cups" in the Passover, and those cups being symbolic of deliverance and redemption, what exactly is "the cup" that Jesus partook of in the Garden of Gethsemane?

In many Old Testament scripture passages, the consequence for sin is likened to drinking from "the cup of [the Lord's] fury."[17] The psalmist explains: "For in the hand of the Lord *there is a cup*, and the wine is red; it is full of mixture; and he poureth out of the same: but the dregs thereof, all the wicked of the earth shall wring them out, and drink them."[18] The "dregs" of the cup is the sediment at the bottom, the strongest concentration of the brew, and therefore, the most bitter.

Ezekiel speaks of this cup as it is given into the hands of Israel as a consequence of her betrayal of her covenants, a cup he describes as "deep and large," and that "containeth much." He calls it the cup of "astonishment and desolation" and testifies that as she drinks from it, she recoils with pain and shock.[19]

Justice demands that each of us drink from the cup of our own making: a cup made up of the bitterness, the shame and guilt of our failures and sins.[20]

While it is true that we often experience bitter consequences as a result of our failures, and ancient Israel was indeed smitten, as prophesied, Isaiah records a promise of Christ's *mercy* when it comes to the cup of wrath:

> *Thus saith thy Lord*
> *the Lord, and thy God that pleadeth the cause of his people,*
> **Behold, I have taken out of thine hand the cup of trembling,**
> **even the dregs of the cup of my fury;**
> **thou shalt no more drink it again.**[21]

Jesus removed the "cup of trembling" from the hand of His people, *and drank from it Himself.*[22] The law of justice demands that the cup be drained, even to its bitter dregs—and Jesus, in mercy, did this for us, *if we will repent and partake of His Atonement.* If we choose not to repent, we must partake of the cup ourselves:

> *For behold, I, God, have suffered these things for all,*
> *that they might not suffer if they would repent;*
> *But if they would not repent they must suffer even as I;*[23]

Each week, we have an opportunity to exchange cups with our Redeemer, Jesus Christ. We symbolically hand Him our own bitter cup, and He gives us a cup of fresh, pure water as we covenant with Him to always remember Him, to keep His commandments, and to live by His Spirit.[24] The Doctrine and Covenants teaches us that justification and sanctification are possible "through the grace of our Lord and Savior Jesus Christ . . . to all those who love and serve God with all their mights, minds, and strength."[25] Jesus's drinking of the cup intended for *us* entitles Him to a special place in the presence of the Father—and in our lives.

> *Listen to him who is the advocate with the Father,*
> *who is pleading your cause before him—Saying:*
> *Father, behold the sufferings and death of him who did no sin,*
> *in whom thou wast well pleased;*
> *behold the blood of thy Son which was shed,*
> *the blood of him whom thou gavest that thyself might be glorified;*
> *Wherefore, Father, spare these my brethren*
> *that believe on my name,*
> *that they may come unto me and have everlasting life.*[26]

Jesus reminds us that His mission and Atonement were all in fulfillment of the *Father's* plan, and He directs our thoughts and hearts constantly towards the Father.[27] Jesus's mission is to bring us back into the presence of the Father, and Their unity of purpose is underscored in the Savior's Intercessory Prayer as recorded by John.[28] Four separate times in that short record, the Savior pleads that those who accept and follow Him may "be one": "I in them, and thou in me, that they may be made perfect in one; and that the world may know that thou hast sent me, and hast loved them, as thou hast loved me."[29] This earnest desire for "oneness" is also repeated in Jesus's prayer amongst the Nephites, a prayer so profoundly sacred, that like the prayer in Gethsemane, we only have a portion of it.[30] While we only have a portion of each of those prayers, it must be significant that what we *do* have emphasizes this desire for unity so frequently!

Elder D. Todd Christofferson explained that:

Jesus achieved perfect unity with the Father by submitting Himself, both flesh and spirit, to the will of the Father. His ministry was always focused because there was no debilitating or distracting double-mindedness in Him. Referring to His Father, Jesus said, "I do always those things that please him.'"[31] . . .

These statements reveal that the Savior's overarching ambition is to glorify the Father. The Father is "in" the Son in the sense that the Father's glory and the Father's will are the all-consuming occupation of the Son.

. . . Surely we will not be one with God and Christ until we make Their will and interest our greatest desire. Such submissiveness is not reached in a day, but through the Holy Spirit, the Lord will tutor us if we are willing until, in process of time, it may accurately be said that He is in us as the Father is in Him.[32]

As Jesus suffered and wept in the Garden, Peter, James, and John kept falling asleep, although they were meant to stay awake and watch as special witnesses of Christ's agony and Atonement in behalf of His people. Jesus had told them He was going to die,[33] and their own hearts were heavy-laden with depression. In His great extremity, and surely feeling utterly alone, Jesus asked, "What, could ye not watch with me one hour?"[34] He repeated this on three occasions that night, each time finding them asleep. But, after He had completed His terrible ordeal, and came to them the third time, it is with loving kindness that Jesus told them: "Sleep on now, and take your rest: behold, the hour is at hand, and the Son of man is betrayed into the hands of sinners."[35] Did He sit with them, then, and wait for Judas to come with the guards? How long did He keep watch over his slumbering friends? This loving kindness, after having suffered so painfully, and still waiting to endure more, reveals so much about Jesus's character and nature.

Cynthia Prentice wrote the following:

Leil Shimurim—The Night of Watching

On the night of watching,
Under the fullness of the Passover moon
The night all Israel lifted the Cup of Sanctification and in Celebration
Remembered how God brought them out from under the burden of the Egyptians . . .

He was there, in the garden grove, waiting to be handed over.

On the night of watching,
Under the fullness of the Passover moon
The night all Israel lifted the Cup of Deliverance and in Celebration
Remembered how God delivered them from Bondage . . .

He was there, in the garden grove, waiting to be bound.

On the night of watching,
Under the fullness of the Passover moon

The night all Israel lifted the Cup of Redemption and in Celebration
Remembered how God redeemed them with an Outstretched arm . . .

He was there, in the garden grove, waiting to be betrayed.

On the night of watching,
Under the fullness of the Passover moon
The night all Israel hoped the Messiah . . .the Anointed one
The Deliverer would come . . .

He was there, in the garden grove, waiting to be captured.

On the night of watching,
Under the fullness of the Passover moon
The night all Israel lifted the Cup of Protection and in celebration
Remembered how God became their God, how he took them as His own,
How he spared their firstborn . . .

The Firstborn of Creation declined the protection. He would not be passed over.
He set the cup down.

On the night of watching,
Under the fullness of the Passover moon
The night all Israel poured the Cup of Elijah, the Cup of God's Wrath, the Cup all left
untouched,
He was there, in the garden grove, with his face to the ground.

On that mountainside,
In the olive grove,
Of the heavy stone, used to crack and crush and squeeze the fruit,
The Geth-semane, that pressed the flesh to bring forth the oil,
He was pressed, as He prayed
Drops of sweat fell like blood to the ground.

Three times he cried, —"Father, if willing, take this cup from Me . . . yet not My will,
But Yours be done."

The cup in his hand was the cup meant for me
My sins were the weight that pressed as he prayed
That night I was rescued, protected, Passed over
He took the cup . . .

And drank it for me.[36]

1 Schalk_and_Elsa, "A night of watching . . . a study of Exodus 12:42," www.setapartpeople.com.

2 Mark 14:32, Joseph Smith Translation.

3 Doctrine and Covenants 19:19.

4 Matthew 26:38.

5 Matthew 26:40; Luke 22:45.

6 Mark 14:43, Joseph Smith Translation.

7 John 13:1.

8 John 15:13.

9 Abraham 3:27.

10 Revelation 13:8.

11 Matthew 26:39; Luke 22:43–44, Joseph Smith Translation.

12 Talmage, *Jesus the Christ*, 613.

13 Doctrine and Covenants 19:18–19.

14 2 Nephi 9:7; Alma 34:12.

15 Doctrine and Covenants 19:19; Maxwell, "Plow in Hope," Apr. 2001 General Conference.

16 Maxwell, "Enduring Well," April 1997 General Conference.

17 Isaiah 51:17.

18 Psalm 75:8.

19 See Ezekiel 23:30–34.

20 See Mosiah 3:26.

21 Isaiah 51:22, emphasis added.

22 See Matthew 26.

23 Doctrine and Covenants 19:16–17.

24 See Doctrine and Covenants 20:79.

25 Doctrine and Covenants 20:30–31.

26 Doctrine and Covenants 45:3–5.

27 See John 16.

28 See John 17.

29 John 17:23; see also verses 11, 21–22.

30 See 3 Nephi 19:23, 29.

31 John 8:29.

32 Christofferson, "That They May Be One in Us," Oct. 2002 General Conference.

33 Matthew 16:21.

34 Matthew 26:40.

35 Matthew 26:45.

36 Prentice, "The Night of Watching."

—⟨∾⚭∾⟩—

CHAPTER 13

The Lamb Is Slain

Think not that I am come to destroy the law, or the prophets:
I am not come to destroy, but to fulfil.
For verily I say unto you, Till heaven and earth pass,
one jot or one tittle shall in no wise pass from the law, till all be fulfilled.[1]

And behold, this is the whole meaning of the law,
every whit pointing to that great and last sacrifice;
and that great and last sacrifice will be the Son of God,
yea infinite and eternal.[2]

To this end was I born, for this cause came I into the world.[3]

A JOT AND A TITTLE ARE TINY PUNCTUATION MARKS, SUCH AS THE dot to an i, or the cross bar to the t. Jesus intends to fulfill every aspect of prophecy, down to the smallest detail, including the specific rituals and details of the ancient feast days.

Many have wondered what Jesus meant in the Garden of Gethsemane when He asked His Father if the cup might be removed from Him.[4] Was there ever a moment when He considered *not* performing that which He had set out to do? Even at the tender age of twelve, He had proclaimed that He "must be about [His] Father's business."[5] While He *was* capable of experiencing the same temptations that all mortals do, including the temptation to turn aside from His mission, Jesus "gave no heed to them."[6] He had dismissed the earlier attempts of Satan's head-on confrontation, and come away victor.[7] Was there any doubt of His victory now? Jesus had consistently told His apostles what lay ahead for Him,[8] and even when Peter fought to protect Him as they left the Garden, Jesus chastened: "Put up thy sword into the sheath: the cup which my Father hath given me, shall I not drink of it?"[9]

Within hours of asking that the cup be removed in Gethsemane, Jesus told Peter that He must continue to partake of it, that "the scriptures must be fulfilled."[10] We do not observe any wavering on His part, and we can really only *guess at* the implications of His plea in the Garden. The full conversation that took place between Jesus and the Father, or Jesus and the angel, is unknown to us, and therefore much of our interpretation of what Jesus meant in asking that the cup pass is simply conjecture.

The bitter cup which had caused such suffering in Gethsemane had still yet to be drained. The long night in the hands of the priests, and the following day of humiliation, scourging, and crucifixion in the hands of the Romans were also part of its contents, and as has been stated, he must drink it to its dregs.

Jesus did not seem to demonstrate any hesitation about meeting His fate. In fact, we read that "knowing all things that should come upon him," Jesus *went forth* to meet Judas and the Temple guards who had come to arrest Him. He did not meekly hide in a corner, hoping that they would not find Him. Rather, in commanding tones He demanded: "Whom seek ye?" When they answered "Jesus of Nazareth," His reply shocked them, and they fell to the ground. His simple three-word response was magisterial: "I am he."[11] A number of Biblical scholars believe that what he actually said was: "I AM he." The Jews knew the name I AM to be the name of their God, Jehovah, given to Moses on the Mount.[12] That name was not spoken lightly, demanded reverence, and would explain why the guards fell back when Jesus said it. Jesus, who *is* Jehovah, did not speak the name in meekness. Isaiah had prophesied that the Messiah would "set his face like a flint" in determination to fulfill His mission,[13] and we can surely see that determination in Jesus's demeanor throughout the two-day period of His agony and torture.

Elder Russell M. Nelson taught the following:

> While visiting the British Museum in London one day, I read a most unusual book. It is not scripture. It is an English translation of an

ancient Egyptian manuscript. From it, I quote a dialogue between the Father and the Son. Referring to His Father, Jehovah—the premortal Lord—says:

"He took the clay from the hand of the angel, and made Adam according to Our image and likeness, and He left him lying for forty days and forty nights without putting breath into him. And He heaved sighs over him daily, saying, 'If I put breath into this [man], he must suffer many pains.' And I said unto My Father, 'Put breath into him; I will be an advocate for him.' And My Father said unto Me, 'If I put breath into him, My beloved Son, Thou wilt be obliged to go down into the world, and to suffer many pains for him before Thou shalt have redeemed him, and made him to come back to his primal state.' And I said unto My Father, 'Put breath into him; I will be his advocate, and I will go down into the world, and will fulfil Thy command.'"

Although this text is not scripture, it reaffirms scriptures that teach of the deep and compassionate love of the Father for the Son, and of the Son for us—attesting that Jesus volunteered willingly to be our Savior and Redeemer.[14]

When the chief priests took Jesus to Pilate for trial, they stated their intention bluntly, and without embarrassment. Pilate had asked them why they did not judge Him themselves according to their own law, and they answered, "[Because] it is not lawful for us to put any man to death."[15] Jewish law *did* permit them to stone a man for blasphemy—their own accusation against Jesus—but they sought for the more shameful death that only the Romans could inflict: crucifixion. Jewish tradition held that "cursed is [he] that hangeth on a tree."[16] Because Jesus had "made himself the Son of God,"[17] the priests intended to humiliate Him to the point where no Jew could ever believe that He was the promised Messiah. The cross of wood upon which He would die would ensure their purposes. Ever after, the way in which He died would be a deterrent to belief. As Paul proclaimed: "But we preach Christ *crucified*; unto the Jews a stumblingblock, and unto the Greeks foolishness."[18]

Romans were not concerned about how or what people worshipped; they had plenty of gods in their own pantheon, and even their emperors were worshipped as gods. Pilate would not have been moved to punish Jesus because He said He was the Son of God. Knowing this, the priests carefully crafted their allegations when presenting their case to Pilate. "If he were not a malefactor, we would not have delivered him up unto thee."[19] *This* charge *would* get Pilate's attention: as the Governor of Judea, it was his responsibility to put down any insurrection. There had been numerous riots amongst the Jews already, and Pilate was on his guard.[20] However, upon examination, Pilate could find no fault in Jesus. Hoping to set Him free, Pilate turned to the Jews and asked: Ye have a custom that I should release unto you one at the Passover: will ye therefore that I release unto you the King of the Jews (Jesus)? But they all cried out: "Not this man . . . but Barabbas"—a man who, ironically, was being held for insurrection and murder.[21] (Another ironical twist is that the name, Bar-Abbas, means "Son of the Father.")

In what appears to be a further attempt to soften the hearts of the people, Pilate had Jesus taken to be scourged. While undergoing this torture, He was mocked by the Roman soldiers, who pressed a crown of thorns upon His head, put a purple robe upon His shoulders, spat upon Him, and smote Him with their hands.[22] Elder Neal A. Maxwell said of the event:

> He was scourged, most likely with a Roman flagellum of several thongs; at the end of each were sharp objects designed to tear the flesh. His tensed back muscles would have been torn. If he was struck with the usual number of blows, 39, the first blows would have bruised and the last blows would have shredded His flesh. Believing Christian physicians wrote that, medically speaking, Jesus would have been in serious, if not critical, medical condition because of the loss of blood; and, as we know by revelation, He had previously bled from every pore in the Garden of Gethsemane.[23]

Following the awful ordeal, Pilate presented Jesus before the people: "Behold the man!"[24] Jesus must have presented a pathetic sight: bloody and torn, the Lamb of God stood before the people who would demand His sacrifice. But they had no pity; even the Roman Governor had more empathy than they did: "Crucify him, crucify him," they cried.[25] In their hatred, they confessed their real purpose to

Pilate: "Because he made himself the Son of God!"[26] This accusation caused Pilate to become even "more afraid," for he had already heard his wife's premonitions concerning any involvement with this Man.[27] Taking Jesus back into the judgment hall, Pilate queried: "Whence art thou? But Jesus gave him no answer. Then saith Pilate unto him, Speakest thou not unto me? Knowest thou not that I have power to crucify thee, and have power to release thee? Jesus answered, Thou couldest have no power against me, except it were given thee from above."[28] Earlier, He had told Pilate: *"To this end was I born, and for this cause came I into the world . . ."*[29]

The die was cast; the outcome sure. In their urgent desire for His death, the people cried out that Pilate need not fear personal responsibility; "His blood be on us, and our children," they shouted.[30] Pilate, in a last act of appeal to the mob, washed his hands before them, signifying that he was clean from any fault.[31] President Thomas S. Monson exclaimed: "Oh foolish, spineless Pilate! Did you really believe that water could cleanse such guilt?"[32] We have to wonder if Pilate wrote his *own* testimony over the cross of Jesus—or was his last act in this matter one of disdain for the people who had brought it all about? Written over every criminal's head was the reason for their execution; Pilate had written, "JESUS OF NAZARETH, THE KING OF THE JEWS" in three languages. When the outraged priests asked him to change the sign to read, "*he said*, I am King of the Jews," Pilate answered them: "What I have written I have written."[33]

The last events of Jesus's mortality were rushing headlong to their awful conclusion. The priests, who had made their accusations before Pilate, must accomplish their murderous desires with dreadful urgency. They must soon return to the temple, where the first morning sacrifice must be completed by 9:00 a.m. Note that the morning and evening sacrifices took place daily, and were distinct from the Passover sacrifices, which Mosaic Law decreed could be offered as early as 12:30 p.m., with the last lamb to be slain and offered between 2:30–3:00 p.m.

The fact that Jerusalem was thronged with Jewish pilgrims from throughout the Roman Empire necessitated haste and diligence on the part of the priests in performing all of their responsibilities before the allotted time had passed. The priests, themselves, would offer their own lambs last of all, and then having completed their duties, would celebrate the Passover together with their families and friends. Complicating their schedule was the fact that the Feast of Unleavened Bread would begin at sundown, when they must gather together once again to present the "Chagigah" or "wave offering" of the first grains of the field before Jehovah and His altar. All of these ceremonies must be performed with exactness, and before witnesses.[34]

The Apostle John states that it was "about the sixth hour," or noon, when Pilate brought Jesus to stand before the angry mobs, hoping that His pathetic appearance would provoke their sympathies.[35] "Behold your King!" he cried, but their hearts were not moved. They demanded His crucifixion, and Pilate, hoping to avoid a riot, complied with their wishes. Luke adds that darkness began to cover "all the earth" at this same time (noon) until "the ninth hour," or 3:00 p.m.[36]

The time-keeping, as recorded in the New Testament, is problematic. John, as stated above, records that it was the sixth hour, or noon, when Pilate presented Jesus to the people, but Mark records that Jesus was on the cross at the third hour, or 9:00 a.m.[37] What we know for certain is that the cock crew outside of Caiaphas's palace, and between that time and the crucifixion, Jesus was taken to Pilate, to Herod, back to Pilate, to flogging, and once again to Pilate before the mob. We also know that the first morning sacrifice in the temple took place by 9:00 a.m., with ritualistic washings, prayers, and the slaying of the lamb to take place beforehand. We also know from all of the gospel writers that darkness covered the land from noon onward, and that Jesus willingly gave up the spirit at 3:00.

Elder Bruce R. McConkie stated in his last testimony, "The Purifying Power of Gethsemane," that Jesus was placed upon the cross at 9:00 a.m., concurring with Mark's account.[38]

If Jesus were condemned in the early morning hours, as Mark and Elder McConkie suggest, the priests would have had *just* enough time to run back to the temple, which was adjacent to the Antonia Fortress, where Jesus was most likely flogged and presented to the people. They could have slipped into their robes, performed their ritual hand washing, and begun the first morning sacrifice at just about the same time that Jesus was being nailed to the cross. The ritual prayer said with the hand washing was in complete contradiction to their previous cry of

"His blood be upon us, and upon our children!"[39] As they carefully washed, they recited the words: "Forgive it to Thy people Israel, whom Thou hast redeemed, O Lord, and lay not innocent blood upon Thy people Israel!"[40]

A note about the throngs in the courtyard who called for Jesus's death. It has been assumed for millennia that thousands of Jews clamored for Jesus's crucifixion, but it is worth considering that if Jesus were put on the cross at 9:00 a.m., as would be fitting in order to fulfill every "jot and tittle"—the first regular morning sacrifice (not a Passover sacrifice) had to be slain at 9:00—then most of the citizens would be in bed sleeping, as they had stayed awake all night for the "Night of Watchings." As the duty to stay awake fell specifically on the men, this might also explain why it was primarily women who wept and followed Jesus to Calvary.

There is no question that the high priests Annas and Caiaphas felt threatened by Jesus's influence over the people, and His stated abhorrence of their setting up markets in the temple. The accounts that have been included here make it clear that the priests—probably Annas and Caiaphas—were leading the fray. But there is nothing to suggest that *all* of the priests were determined to kill Jesus, nor is there anything to confirm that the majority of the citizens of Jerusalem demanded that Jesus be put to death. Accusations such as these are only efforts to pass the blame from our own shoulders, and have led to terrible persecution of the Jews by Christians for thousands of years. It's unfair and un-Christian to take such a view. Instead of seeking to place blame on others, it would be wiser for us to have the attitude of the Apostles who asked, "Is it I?"[41] when Jesus told them that one of them would betray Him. Each one of us is responsible for the Atonement of Christ, and each one of us needs that Atonement. Elder Dieter Uchtdorf counseled: "In these simple words, 'Lord, is it I?' lies the beginning of wisdom and the pathway to personal conversion and lasting change."[42]

Both Luke and Mark record that Jesus cried out to His Father and died at the "ninth hour" (3:00 p.m.) and that the temple veil was rent from top to bottom at that same moment.[43] This ninth hour of Christ's death is called "the hour of prayer" in the temple.[44] At the very moment when Jesus cried out and entered within the veil of the *actual* "Holy of Holies," a priest would have stood before the veil of the temple, offering incense and pleading in behalf of the people: "True it is that Thou art Jehovah our God, . . . our Saviour and the Saviour of our fathers; our Maker and the Rock of our salvation; our Help and our Deliverer . . . Jehovah shall reign who saveth Israel . . . Appoint peace, goodness, and blessing; grace, mercy, and compassion for us, and for all Israel Thy people. *Bless us, O our Father, all of us as one, with the light of Thy countenance.* For in the light of Thy countenance hast Thou, Jehovah, our God, given us the law of life, and loving mercy, and righteousness, and blessing, and compassion, and life, and peace . . ."[45]

At that hour, as the prayer was recited, the last sacrificial lambs would be burning on the altar in the outer courts. The courts would be full of worshippers, kneeling before the temple, all with the single plea in their hearts and voices: "Let us behold the face of Jehovah the Messiah." Pondering these exquisite and ironic details must provoke a number of responses: horror at the blindness of Jehovah's appointed stewards, awe at the precision with which prophecy is fulfilled, pity and sorrow for *both* the people and the Savior, and self-examination of our own abilities of perception and discipleship. Perhaps, in order to come to an understanding of the Atonement, we must pause and figuratively kneel in the Garden and at the Cross with our Lord, who in some miraculous way, met with each one of us there so many years ago. These events deserve more than our contemplation; they require our all as we pour out our soul seeking for understanding.[46]

What we see will cause us pain; if we are successful, it will break our hearts. True salvation requires nothing less:

> *Behold, he offereth himself a sacrifice for sin,*
> *to answer the ends of the law,*
> *unto all those who have a broken heart and a contrite spirit;*
> *and unto none else can the ends of the law be answered.*[47]

Death by crucifixion was brutal and tortuous. Public humiliation was part of the ordeal, as Jesus stumbled through jeering crowds who were eager to make a festival out of His death. Even as He hung in agony, many came out from the city to stand, jeer, and mock. There were, however, faithful women who mourned and lamented.

Jesus, who noticed all, even in the midst of His suffering, counseled: "Daughters of Jerusalem, weep not for me, but weep for yourselves, and for your children."[48] Many of the women followed Him through the streets, watching all that transpired, and stood in grief and pity at the foot of His cross. Amongst them were "the Marys": His mother, Mary Magdalene, and Mary, the wife of Cleophas.[49] They would not desert Him, and although they had looked so often to *Him* for comfort, now they offered all that they had to give with the desire to ease *His* sufferings. A woman's natural instinct recoils from violence and cruelty; knowing this, we realize what it must have taken for them to be there with Jesus. He had brought new light and new life to womanhood. Did these women who loved Him so, stroke His legs and feet, offering words of comfort? As they did so, did His blood spill over upon their hands and clothing, even their upturned faces?

Neal A. Maxwell wrote:

> The necessary but awesome shedding of Jesus's blood thus occurred not only in the severe scourging, but earlier in Gethsemane. A recent and thoughtful article by several physicians on the physical death of Jesus Christ indicates that "the severe scourging, with its intense pain and appreciable blood loss, most probably left Jesus in a preshock state." (We all recall, of course, that a dramatically weakened Jesus needed help to carry the cross.) "Therefore, even before the actual crucifixion, Jesus's physical condition was at least serious and possibly critical. . . . Although scourging may have resulted in considerable blood loss, crucifixion per se was a relatively bloodless procedure."[50]

As a 21st-century society, we recoil from the sight of blood, but blood held tremendous significance for those of ancient days, and above all on the Passover, as the sacrificial lambs were drained completely of blood before they were taken to individual homes.

The Lord had instructed:

> *For the life of the flesh is the blood:*
> *and I have given it to you upon the altar*
> *to make an atonement for your souls:*
> *for it is the blood that maketh an atonement for the soul.*[51]

The blood spilled upon the altar, taken into the Holy of Holies and applied to the Mercy Seat of the Ark of the Covenant was a constant visual reminder. Imagine watching the priests with their silver and golden bowls throwing the blood "in one jet" to the base of the altar at Passover![52] These symbols were foreshadowing Christ's sacrifice. It took a great deal of blood to cover and atone for our sins. This blood Jesus shed freely—in *every* sense of that term. Even as Jesus did not shrink from partaking of the bitter cup, let us not shrink from contemplating the very "bloodiness" of His Atonement, for we are instructed that only those who have "washed their garments in the blood of the Lamb" can be saved.[53] We must also drink from the sacrament cup in remembrance of His blood.[54]

The Passover recitation in which all participants join exclaims: *"By the blood of the Lamb are we saved! By the blood of the Lamb was death made to pass over!"*

Even while His blood ran, and His life ebbed, Jesus looked with love upon those around Him. Faithful John also stood at the cross, and into his care the Lord committed His beloved mother.[55]

He also shared words of kindness for the Roman soldiers: "Father forgive them, for they know not what they do,"[56] and the repentant thief at His side: "This day thou shalt be with me in paradise."[57]

As cruel as the cross was, Jesus's greatest agony came when the Father withdrew His Spirit, and He was left alone in His suffering. Earlier in His ministry He had said: "He that sent me is with me: the Father hath not left me alone; for I do always those things that please him."[58] Their unity was perfect, and Jesus depended upon it. Note, also, the innocent and forthright explanation of "for I do always those things that please him." This loving submission on Jesus's part, this overwhelming desire of His heart ensured the bonds of love and unity between the Father and the Son. Their goals and work were in perfect alignment: "to bring to pass the immortality and eternal life of man."[59]

President Brigham Young's insight helps us understand Jesus's aloneness, which was a unique dimension of His agony:

At the very moment, at the hour when the crisis came for him to offer up his life, the Father withdrew Himself, withdrew His Spirit, and cast a veil over [Jesus]. That is what made him sweat blood. If he had had the power of God upon him, he would not have sweat blood; but all was withdrawn from him, and a veil was cast over him, and he then plead with the Father not to forsake him.[60]

President Young's statement implies that the Savior underwent a recurrence of the Garden experience while on the cross, and Elder McConkie confirmed: ". . . while He was hanging on the cross . . . all the infinite agonies and merciless pains of Gethsemane recurred.[61]

If Jesus, as Savior, had to "descend below all things,"[62] He must also experience the withdrawal of the Spirit that comes with sin. As a proxy for sinners, He no longer felt the approbation that comes to a Son who "does all things to please His Father." We can only imagine how the Father must have felt as He turned away from His Beloved Son . . . the only One who obeyed in all things and with perfect submission.

The last words the Savior uttered from the cross were: "It is finished: Father, into thy hands I commend my spirit."[63] He willingly gave His life; no man had power to take it from Him. As He had earlier said, "Therefore doth my Father love me, because I lay down my life, that I might take it again. No man taketh it from me, but I lay it down of myself. I have power to lay it down, and I have power to take it again. This commandment have I received of my Father."[64] And, later, as He explained to the Nephites:

And my Father sent me that I might be lifted up upon the cross;
and after that I had been lifted up upon the cross,
that I might draw all men unto me . . .[65]

Paul taught that Jesus/Jehovah, officiating in His capacity as the Great High Priest, offered His prayer to the Father in similitude of the prayer being offered by the priest in the temple at the hour of prayer: "Open the veil to Thy people, that they may enter into Thy presence." Expressing His prayer from the cross, with His arms outstretched (even as the priest within the temple would be standing), Jesus performed what no earthly priest could: through His sacrifice He provided the way for us to return through the veil and into the presence of the Father. Paul wrote:

For Christ is not entered into the holy places made with hands,
which are the figures of the true;
but into heaven itself,
now to appear in the presence of God for us . . .
Having therefore, brethren,
boldness to enter into the holiest by the blood of Jesus,
By a new and living way, which he hath consecrated for us,
through the veil, that is to say, his flesh;[66]

The rending of the veil is understood, then, in a new light: Jesus Christ has opened it everlastingly to those who will follow Him.

As sundown approached, the Jewish elders became concerned lest the Jewish bodies still on the crosses would desecrate the coming Sabbath. They asked Pilate's permission to speed their deaths by breaking their legs (making it so that they could not stand against the cross brace, thereby hurrying death by suffocation caused by the weight of the body folding in against the lungs). When the soldiers approached Jesus, they found that He had already died, but to be sure, they pierced his side with a spear. From the wound flowed water and blood, evidence that Jesus's heart had actually burst, or ruptured. Medical experts agree that only "great mental stress, poignant emotion either of grief or joy, and intense spiritual struggle are among the recognized causes of heart rupture."[67]

Not a bone was to be broken in the preparations of the Passover Lamb. Jesus, the Lamb of God, despite the horrible ordeal of flogging and crucifixion, had no broken bones.

Wherefore, how great the importance
to make these things known unto the inhabitants of the earth,
that they may know that there is no flesh
that can dwell in the presence of God,
save it be through the merits, and mercy,
and grace of the Holy Messiah,
who layeth down his life according to the flesh,
and taketh it again by the power of the Spirit . . .
Wherefore, he is the firstfruits unto God,
inasmuch as he shall make intercession for all the children of men . . ."[68]

The most important aspect of the Atonement is in how it pertains to us individually, and personally. We may be able to list all of the illegalities of the trials, or debate as to whether Judas was prompted by Satan, or simply fulfilling a foreordained mission, but unless we feel the profound weight of the suffering Jesus bore because of *our* sins, afflictions, and sorrows, we really don't know anything about what salvation means. Elder George Q. Morris stated: "The principle question before us is not do we comprehend the atonement, but do we accept it and know that it is true."[69]

What does it mean to accept the Atonement of Jesus Christ? We must first admit that we stand in *need* of it!

> *Wherefore, all mankind were in a lost and in a fallen state, and ever would be save they should rely on this Redeemer.*[70]

> *Yea, remember that there is no other way nor means whereby man can be saved, only through the atoning blood of Jesus Christ.*[71]

In our current world, based upon relativism, we must admit the concrete fact that without Jesus's gift of grace, we are unclean and unworthy to enter the presence of God. As Jesus humbled Himself for our sakes, we must humble ourselves before Him, and admit that without Him we are nothing.[72] Let us not, as so many others do, stumble at the cross, or the Garden, excusing any lack of belief or adoration. *Let us not explain away the terrible suffering Jesus, in fact, experienced in our behalf.*

Elder James E. Talmage wrote:

> In that hour of anguish Christ met and overcame all the horrors that Satan, "the prince of this world" could inflict. The frightful struggle incident to the temptations immediately following the Lord's baptism was surpassed and overshadowed by this supreme contest with the powers of evil."[73]

Alfred Edersheim adds:

> His going into Death was His final conflict with Satan for man, and on his behalf. By submitting to it He took away the power of Death; He disarmed Death by burying his shaft in His own Heart. And beyond this lies the deep, unutterable mystery of Christ

bearing the penalty due to our sin, bearing our death, bearing the penalty of the broken Law, the accumulated guilt of humanity, and the holy wrath of the Righteous Judge upon them.[74]

Nothing compares to the atoning sacrifice of our Lord. It is the most important single event that has ever occurred in the entire history of created things; it is the bedrock foundation upon which the gospel and all other things rest. Indeed, as the prophet Joseph Smith said, "All things which pertain to our religion are only appendages to it."[75]

---

1 Matthew 5:17–18.
2 Alma 34:14.
3 John 18:37.
4 Mark 14:36.
5 Luke 2:49.
6 Doctrine and Covenants 20:22.
7 Matthew 4:1–10.
8 Matthew 20:19.
9 John 18:11.
10 Mark 14:49.
11 John 18:4–6.
12 Exodus 3:14.
13 Isaiah 50:7.
14 Nelson, "The Creation," Apr. 2000 General Conference.
15 John 18:28–31.
16 Galatians 3:13; Deuteronomy 21:23.
17 John 19:7.
18 1 Corinthians 1:23.
19 John 18:30; Luke 23:2, 5.
20 See Acts 5:36–37.
21 John 18:38–40; Mark 15:7.
22 John 19:1–3; Matthew 27:27–30.
23 Maxwell, "Enduring Well," Apr. 1997 *Ensign*.
24 John 19:5.
25 Luke 23:21.
26 John 19:6–7.
27 Matthew 27:19.
28 John 19:5–11.
29 John 18:37.
30 Matthew 27:25.
31 Matthew 27:24–25.
32 Monson, "Hands," August 1990 *Ensign*.
33 John 19:19–22.
34 See Edersheim, *The Temple: Its Ministry and Services*, 148–70.
35 John 19:14.
36 Luke 23:44.

37 Mark 15:25.

38 McConkie, "The Purifying Power of Gethsemane," Apr. 1985 General Conference.

39 Matthew 27:25.

40 Edersheim, *The Life and Times of Jesus the Messiah*, 873.

41 Matthew 26:22.

42 Uchtdorf, "Lord, Is It I?" Oct. 2014 General Conference.

43 Mark 15:34–38; Luke 23:44–46.

44 Acts 3:1.

45 Edersheim, *The Temple: Its Ministry and Services*, 128–31.

46 Isaiah 53:12; Psalm 42:4; Alma 34:26.

47 2 Nephi 2:.

48 Luke 23:27–28.

49 John 19:25.

50 Maxwell, "'Overcome . . . Even As I Also Overcame,'" Apr. 1987 General Conference.

51 Leviticus 17:11.

52 See Edersheim, *The Temple: Its Ministry and Services*, 175–76.

53 Revelation 7:14; Alma 13:11.

54 Doctrine and Covenants 20:79.

55 John 19:26–27.

56 Luke 23:24, Joseph Smith Translation.

57 Matthew 27:44, Joseph Smith Translation.

58 John 8:29.

59 Moses 1:39.

60 *Journal of Discourses,* 3:206., as quoted in Maxwell, "Enduring Well."

61 McConkie, "The Purifying Power of Gethsemane," Apr. 1985 General Conference.

62 Doctrine and Covenants 88:6.

63 John 19:30; Luke 23; 46.

64 John 10:17–18.

65 3 Nephi 27:14.

66 Hebrews 9:24, 10:19–21.

67 Talmage, *Jesus the Christ*, 621.

68 2 Nephi 2:8–9.

69 Morris, "The Meaning of the Atonement," in Conference Report, Apr. 1956, 112.

70 1 Nephi 10:6.

71 Helaman 5:9.

72 John 15:5.

73 Talmage, *Jesus the Christ*, 569.

74 Edersheim, *The Life and Times of Jesus the Messiah*, 846.

75 *Teachings of the Prophet Joseph Smith*, 121.

CHAPTER 14

The Passover, *Seder*, or Order

THE FOLLOWING RITUALS AND ITEMS ARE SOMEWHAT UNIVERSAL to all Passover celebrations. They are included in what is called the *Seder*, or order of the Passover.

Commentaries have been added below in each section in order to help illustrate the connection between the ritual and the life and atonement of Jesus Christ.

PROLOGUE TO THE FEAST— THE SEARCH FOR, AND REMOVAL OF ALL LEAVEN

We have previously discussed that it was the role of the father of the household to search for any hidden leaven, to remove it, and to burn it with fire. The father would use a candle to peer into every corner of the house with a wooden spoon and a feather to gather any hidden particles. The leaven, or yeast, represented anything that might ferment, spoil, or corrupt the host.

Paul wrote: "Your glorying is not good. Know ye not that a little leaven leaveneth the whole lump? Purge out therefore the old leaven, that ye may be a new lump, as ye are unleavened. For even Christ our passover is sacrificed for us: Therefore let us keep the feast, not with old leaven, neither with the leaven of malice and wickedness; but with the unleavened bread of sincerity and truth."[1]

Referring to the Second Coming, the Lord warns:

And it shall come to pass at that time, that I will search Jerusalem with candles, and punish the men that are settled on their lees [complacent or indifferent]: *that say in their heart, The Lord will not do good, neither will he do evil.²*

Will Jesus find any leaven in our hearts or homes when He searches us?

LIGHTING OF THE CANDLES

A woman lights the candles and recites the same blessing given by the priest at the temple following the burning of the incense: "The Lord bless thee, and keep thee: the Lord make his face shine upon thee, and be gracious unto thee: The Lord lift up his countenance upon thee, and give thee peace."³

The hope of seeing the Messiah is recited in this prayer and in the daily prayers of the temple. This is the same blessing that Zacharias *would have* pronounced upon the people after burning the incense before the veil *if* he had been able to speak. Gabriel announced to Zacharias that the unified prayer of the priest and the people in the courtyard was about to be answered: The Messiah was coming!⁴

Jesus said:

I am the light of the world: he that followeth me shall not walk in darkness, but shall have the light of life."⁵

I am come a light into the world, that whosoever believeth on me should not abide in darkness.⁶

THE WASHING OF HANDS

Recitation:

The earth is the Lord's, and the fulness thereof; the world, and they that dwell therein.

For he hath founded it upon the seas, and established it upon the floods.

Who shall ascend into the hill of the Lord? or who shall stand in his holy place?

He that hath clean hands, and a pure heart, who hath not lifted up his soul unto vanity nor sworn deceitfully.

He shall receive the blessing from the Lord, and righteousness from the God of his salvation.

This is the generation of them that seek him, that seek thy face, O Jacob.[7]

Scripture Commentary:

He riseth from supper, and laid aside his garments; and took a towel, and girded himself.

After that he poureth water into a bason, and began to wash the disciples' feet, and to wipe them with the towel wherewith he was girded.

Then cometh he to Simon Peter: and Peter saith unto him, Lord, dost thou wash my feet?

Jesus answered and said unto him, What I do thou knowest not now; but thou shalt know hereafter.

Peter saith unto him, Thou shalt never wash my feet. Jesus answered him, If I wash thee not, thou hast no part with me.

Simon Peter saith unto him, Lord, not my feet only, but also my hands and my head.

Jesus saith to him, He that is washed needeth not save to wash his feet, but is clean every whit: and ye are clean, but not all.

For he knew who should betray him; therefore said he, Ye are not all clean.[8]

KARPAS (FRESH HERBS DIPPED IN SALTWATER)

Recitation:

"We will take the parsley, called *kar-pas* and we will dip it into the salt water. We do this to symbolize the tears and pain of the Israelites. After the following prayer, take the parsley and dip it into the salt water and remember that even though we have painful circumstances in our lives, we will always have the hope of God to free us from our tribulations."

Praise:

"Blessed art thou, O Eternal, our God, King of the Universe, Creator of the fruits of the earth."

The parsley represents fruitfulness of hope that God remembers His people. The saltwater represents the tears of His people.

Scriptural Commentary:

He will swallow up death in victory; and the Lord God will wipe away tears from off all faces; and the rebuke of his people shall he take away from off all the earth: for the Lord hath spoken it.[9]

For the Lamb which is in the midst of the throne shall feed them, and shall lead them unto living fountains of waters: and God shall wipe away all tears from their eyes.[10]

And God shall wipe away all tears from their eyes; and there shall be no more death, neither sorrow, nor crying, neither shall there be any more pain: for the former things are passed away.[11]

Breaking of the Bread—The Three Matzahs, The Center Broken and Hidden—The Bread of Affliction

Recitation:

"This is the bread of affliction which our ancestors ate in the land of Egypt; let all those who are hungry, enter and eat thereof; and all who are in distress, come and celebrate the Passover."

We have discussed previously the significance of this part of the Passover ritual.[12] Jesus Christ was "broken" for us. His role as Messiah and Redeemer is often "hidden" until one searches for Him with the faith of a little child. The bread is pressed flat, pierced, and looks "bruised" or "striped." The sacrament bread is broken, or torn, in like manner.

Scriptural Commentary:

He is despised and rejected of men; a man of sorrows, and acquainted with grief: and we hid as it were our faces from him; he was despised, and we esteemed him not.

Surely he hath borne our griefs, and carried our sorrows: yet we did esteem him stricken, smitten of God, and afflicted.

But he was wounded for our transgressions, he was bruised for our iniquities; the chastisement of our peace was upon him; and with his stripes we are healed.[13]

And I will pour upon the house of David, and upon the inhabitants of Jerusalem, the spirit of grace and of supplications: and they shall look upon me whom they have pierced, and they shall mourn for him, as one mourneth for his only son, and shall be in bitterness for him, as one that is in bitterness for his firstborn.[14]

THE FOUR QUESTIONS

The Lord instructed the children of Israel that they were to teach their "sons" to keep the Passover, and to tutor them in its meaning.[15] At this point in the Feast, four questions are asked, usually by the youngest child present. Commentators believe that this part of the Passover would have been spoken by John, who was the youngest of the Twelve.

Wherefore is this night distinguished from all other nights?

1. On all other nights we may eat either leavened or unleavened bread; but on this night why only unleavened bread?
2. On all other nights we may eat herbs of any kind; but on this night why only bitter herbs?
3. On all other nights we do not dip our herbs even once; but on this night why do we dip them twice?
4. On all other nights we eat our meals sitting or reclining; but on this night why do we eat in a reclining position?

Recitation:

"Because we were slaves unto Pharaoh in Egypt, and Jehovah, our God, brought us forth thence with a mighty hand and an outstretched arm. And if the Most Holy, blessed be He, had not brought forth our ancestors from Egypt, we and our children and our children's children would still be in bondage to the Pharaohs in Egypt. We therefore consider it a sacred duty and obligation to keep this miracle of salvation ever alive in our memories."

Commentary:

It is poignant and sobering to contemplate the fact that children throughout Jerusalem were asking these questions as Jesus and His apostles met together for the Last Supper. As the neighbors looked to the past and their miraculous deliverance, they also hoped for a future deliverance from the bondage of Rome. Deliverance *was coming* in a manner they did not expect or look for, and would provide freedom from a power much stronger than Rome's . . . and *this night* would be the night that that rescuing redemption would begin. Jesus provided freedom from bondage not just for a decade, or even a century, but for eternity—if His people would accept it. Rome would still hold its iron fist over future converts, and many would lose their lives, but, like Peter and Paul, they found a liberty they had never even dreamed of in a sure hope of salvation.

Following the four questions, are questions asked by four "sons" who represent varying levels of spiritual maturity: a wise one, a wicked one, a simple one, and one who is unable to ask for himself. Not all are equally equipped to receive the message of Passover; not all are equally sensitive to its importance. The questions they ask about the meaning of Passover and its rituals are different and varied, and must be responded to at the level of their understanding (it appears that Alma may have been following this pattern as he counseled his sons Helaman, Shiblon, and Corianton).[16]

Recitation of the First Passover Story

Recitation:

> *For I will pass through the land of Egypt this night, and will smite all the firstborn in the land of Egypt, both man and beast; and against all the gods of Egypt I will execute judgment: I am the Lord."*
>
> *And the blood (of the lamb) shall be to you for a token upon the houses where ye are: and when I see the blood, I will pass over you, and the plague shall not be upon you to destroy you, when I smite the land of Egypt.*
>
> *And this day shall be unto you for a memorial; and ye shall keep it a feast to the Lord throughout your generations; ye shall keep it a feast by an ordinance for ever.[17]*

All present recite:

"By the blood of the lamb was Israel spared. By the blood of the lamb was Jacob redeemed. By the blood of the lamb was death made to pass over."

Scriptural Commentary:

He was oppressed, and he was afflicted, yet he opened not his mouth: he is brought as a lamb to the slaughter, and as a sheep before her shearers is dumb, so he openeth not his mouth."[18]

All present recite:

"And we cried unto the Eternal, the God of our fathers, and the Eternal heard our voice, saw our affliction, our sorrow, and our oppression. And the Eternal brought us forth from Egypt, with a strong hand and with an outstretched arm, with great terror, and with signs and wonders. And the Eternal brought us forth from Egypt: not by means of an angel, nor by means of a Seraph, nor by means of a messenger; but the most Holy, blessed be He, in His own glory."

Scriptural Commentary:

Then said Jesus unto them again, verily, verily, I say unto you, I am the door of the sheep. . . . I am the door: by me if any man enter in, he shall be saved, and shall go in and out and find pasture.[19]

O then, my beloved brethren, come unto the Lord the Holy One. Remember his paths are righteous. Behold, the way for man is narrow, but it lieth in a straight course before him, and the keeper of the gate is the Holy One of Israel; and he employeth no servant there; and there is none other way save it be by the gate; for he cannot be deceived for the Lord God is his name.[20]

And one of the elders saith unto me, Weep not: behold the Lion of the tribe of Judah, the Root of David, hath prevailed to open the book, and to loose the seven seals thereof.

And I beheld, and, lo, in the midst of the throne and of the four beasts, and in the midst of the elders, stood a Lamb as it had been slain . . .[21]

Even as the blood of those first Passover lambs was applied in faith to the doorposts of Israel's homes, so the blood of the Messiah must be applied in faith to the doorposts of our hearts.

THE THREE SYMBOLS—THE LAMB

Recitation:

"This Paschal lamb, which our ancestors ate during the existence of the Temple – for what reason was it eaten? Because the Holy One, blessed be He, passed over the houses of our ancestors in Egypt, as it is said: 'Ye shall say, it is a sacrifice of the Passover unto the Lord, who passed over the houses of the children of Israel in Egypt.'"

Commentary:

McConkie, in *The Mortal Messiah*, states:

The ordinary evening service and sacrifice in the temple must precede the supper. On this feast day this service began an hour early, or at about 1:30 p.m., with the evening sacrifice itself being offered at about 2:30 p.m. This was the time for the slaying of the Paschal lambs by their owners and the sprinkling of their blood upon the altar by the priests. Both Mark and Luke say that Peter and John were to "make ready" the Passover meal, and they both record that "they made ready the passover." Of necessity this means that the two apostles, rather than the homeowner or some other person, were required to and did attend the temple services for the formal slaying and preparation of the lamb, and to this assumption there is a certain fitness and propriety: two of the chief apostles, for themselves and on behalf of their Lord and their brethren, were complying to the full to the letter of the law on the last day on which its provisions were in force. When, on the morrow, the true Paschal Lamb was slain, the old order would be over and the new covenant only would have binding efficacy and force.[22]

Edersheim further explains:

It was done on this wise: The first of the three festive divisions, with their Paschal lambs, was admitted within the court of the Priests. Each division must consist of not less than thirty persons

(3 X 10, the symbolic number of the Divine and of completeness). Immediately the massive gates were closed behind them. The priests drew a threefold blast from their silver trumpets when the Passover was slain. Altogether the scene was most impressive. All along the Court up to the altar of burnt-offering priests stood in two rows, the one holding golden, the other silver bowls. In these the blood of the Paschal lambs, which each Israelite slew for himself (as representative of his company at the Paschal Suppers), was caught up by a priest, who handed it to his colleague, receiving back an empty bowl, and so the bowls with the blood were passed up to the priest at the altar, who jerked it in one jet at the base of the altar. While this was going on, a most solemn "hymn" of praise was raised, the Levites leading in song, and the offerers either repeating after them or merely responding. This service of song consisted of the so-called "Hallel," which comprised Psalm 113 to 118, working its way to the crescendo for the phrases: "Save now, I beseech thee, O Lord: O Lord, I beseech thee, send now prosperity. Blessed be he that cometh in the name of the Lord: we have blessed you out of the house of the Lord."[23]

The Three Symbols—The Unleavened Bread

Recitation:

"The unleavened bread which we now eat, what does it mean? It is eaten because the dough of our ancestors had not time to become leavened, before the supreme King of kings, the Most Holy, blessed be He! revealed Himself unto them, and they baked unleavened cakes of the dough which they had brought forth out of Egypt, for it was not leavened, because they were thrust out of Egypt, and could not tarry, neither had they made any provision for themselves."

Commentary:

The unleavened bread represents the bricks the Israelites were forced to make in Egypt. Leaving out the leaven from the bread represents removing the spoiling influences of the world. It also reminds the children of Israel that they had to leave Egypt in a hurry. We must cleanse the impurities of the world from our lives, and there is urgency in the commandment to do so.

THE THREE SYMBOLS—THE BITTER HERBS

Recitation:

"This bitter herb which we eat, what does it mean? It is eaten because the Egyptians embittered the lives of our ancestors in Egypt."

The bitterness of sin is the worst form of slavery.

Scriptural Commentary:

Behold, for peace I had great bitterness: but thou hast in love to my soul delivered it from the pit of corruption: for thou hast cast all my sins behind thy back.[24]

My soul hath been redeemed from the gall of bitterness and bonds of iniquity. I was in the darkest abyss; but now I behold the marvelous light of God. My soul was racked with eternal torment, but I am snatched, and my soul is pained no more.[25]

THE THREE SYMBOLS—THE SOP

Recitation:

Break bread and distribute. (Show the bitter herbs to the assembly. Show the Charoseth, or Maror [apple mixture] to the assembly.) "The Charoseth represents the Egyptian mortar. Take the bread, dip it in the bitter herbs and the Charoseth, and eat it, that the scripture may be fulfilled which says: 'They shall eat it [the Passover offering] with matzah and bitter herbs.'"[26]

Commentary:

Edersheim explains:

This sandwich was eaten with lamb during temple times in Jerusalem, it is also known as the sop. It is still the custom today to give this dipped sop with affection to a loved one . . . This, in all probability, was "the sop" which, in answer to John's inquiry about the betrayer, the Lord "gave" to Judas.[27]

Scriptural Commentary:

I speak not of you all: I know whom I have chosen: but that the scripture may be fulfilled, He that eateth bread with me hath lifted up his heel against me.

Now I tell you before it come, that, when it is come to pass, ye may believe that I am he [the Christ]. . . .

When Jesus had thus said, he was troubled in spirit, and testified, and said, Verily, verily, I say unto you, that one of you shall betray me.

Then the disciples looked one on another, doubting of whom he spake.

Now there was leaning on Jesus' bosom one of his disciples, whom Jesus loved.

Simon Peter therefore beckoned to him, that he should ask who it should be of whom he spake.

He then lying on Jesus' breast saith unto him, Lord, who is it?

Jesus answered, He it is, to whom I shall give a sop, when I have dipped it. And when he had dipped the sop, he gave it to Judas Iscariot, the son of Simon.

And after the sop Satan entered into him. Then said Jesus unto him, That thou doest, do quickly."[28]

BLESSING OF THE LAMB

The sacrifice of the lambs would take place in what we would consider a two-day period; but in actuality occurred in a 24-hour period the Jews referred to as "one day." The slaughter and preparation of the lamb had to follow very precise instructions. The lamb's throat was to be cut, and its blood drained into golden and silver bowls near the temple altar. The lamb was then hung on hooks to be skinned. The stomach was cut open to remove the entrails so as not to taint the meat, and the fat and entrails were burned on the altar. The family could then take the lamb home for their Passover table. The lamb was to be roasted whole, without breaking any bones, and the lamb was to be entirely consumed at the Passover meal, with no "leftovers."

The poorer people, who had fewer preparations to make for a feast, would begin their Passover feasts on what we would now call the first day. The priests, who had to officiate in the sacrifices, and the wealthier citizens of the community would finish their sacrifices by 2:30 p.m. of what we would call the second day, ending their duties, and partaking of the Feast before sundown. The hour of prayer was at 3:00 p.m. daily, with all citizens joining in. Thus, Jesus, the Lamb of God, hung on the cross at the time the priests were performing the sacrifices for their own tables, and he gave up His life at 3:00 p.m., the exact time the priest would be standing before the veil and praying in behalf of all of Israel.

SINGING OF THE HALLEL (PSALMS 115–118)

Portions of the Hallel include the following from Psalm 118:

> *"All Thy works shall praise Thee, Jehovah our God. And Thy saints, the righteous, who do Thy good pleasure, and all Thy people, the house of Israel, with joyous song let them praise, and bless, and magnify, and glorify, and exalt, and reverence, and sanctify, and ascribe the kingdom to Thy name, O our King! For it is good to praise Thee, and pleasure to sing praises unto Thy name, for from everlasting to everlasting Thou art God.*
>
> *"The breath of all that lives shall praise Thy name, Jehovah our God. And the spirit of all flesh shall continually glorify and exalt Thy memorial, O our King! For from everlasting to everlasting Thou art God, and besides Thee we have no King, Redeemer or Saviour."*
>
> *"O give thanks unto the Lord; for he is good: because his mercy endureth for ever. Let Israel now say, that his mercy endureth for ever. Let the house of Aaron now say, that his mercy endureth for ever. Let them now that fear the Lord say, that his mercy endureth for ever.*
>
> *"I called upon the Lord in distress: the Lord answered me, and set me in a large place. The Lord is on my side; I will not fear: what can man do unto me?*
>
> *"The Lord is my strength and song, and is become my salvation. The voice of rejoicing and salvation is in the tabernacles of the righteous: the right hand of the Lord doeth valiantly. I shall not die, but live, and declare the*

works of the Lord. The Lord hath chastened me sore: but he hath not given me over unto death.

"Open to me the gates of righteousness: I will go into them, and I will praise the Lord: This gate of the Lord, into which the righteous shall enter. I will praise thee: for thou hast heard me, and art become my salvation.

"The stone which the builders refused is become the head stone of the corner. This is the Lord's doing; it is marvelous in our eyes.

"This is the day which the Lord hath made; we will rejoice and be glad in it. Save now, I beseech thee, O Lord: O Lord, I beseech thee . . . Thou art my God, and I will praise thee: thou art my God, I will exalt thee. O give thanks unto the Lord; for he is good: for his mercy endureth forever."[29]

THE CLOSING OF THE FEAST

Those who celebrate the Passover today have added the following:

"In closing, we call out to our Lord and God, Have compassion, O Lord our God, upon us, upon Israel Your people, upon Jerusalem Your city, on Zion the dwelling place of Your glory, and upon Your altar and Your Temple. Rebuild Jerusalem, Your holy city, speedily in our days. Be gracious to us and give us strength.

"O Pure One in heaven above, restore the congregation of Israel in Your love, speedily lead Your redeemed people to Zion in joy. . . . And all reply: 'Next year in Jerusalem!'"

---

1 1 Corinthians 5:6–8.

2 Zephaniah 1:12.

3 Numbers 6:24–26.

4 See Luke 1:5–17.

5 John 8:12.

6 John 12:46.

7 Psalm 24:1–6

8 John 13:4–11.

9 Isaiah 25:8.

10 Revelation 7:17.

11 Revelation 21:4.

12 See Chapter 9—Jesus at Passover, *Pesach*.

13 Isaiah 53:3–5.

14 Zechariah 12:10.

15 Exodus 13:8.

16 See Alma 36–42.

17 Exodus 12:12–14.

18 Isaiah 53:7.
19 John 10:7, 9.
20 2 Nephi 9:41.
21 Revelation 5:5–6.
22 McConkie, *Mortal Messiah*, 4:25.
23 Edersheim, *The Temple: Its Ministry and Services*, 175–76.
24 Isaiah 38:17.
25 Mosiah 27:29.
26 Exodus 12:8.
27 Edersheim, *The Temple: Its Ministry and Services*, 190.
28 John 13:18–27.
29 Psalm 118: 1–6, 14–29.

CHAPTER 15

———— ❦ ————

Remarkable Passover Celebrations

- With Moses in the Sinai wilderness.[1]
- With Joshua before taking Jericho. The manna from heaven ceased the day after this Passover. Before they could participate in the Passover, all males had to be circumcised, as none had been circumcised since they had left Egypt.[2]
- Under King Hezekiah after he cleansed the land of idols. He invited all Israel to come and celebrate the Passover, for it had not been held for many years. Because the Levites were not clean at the time the Passover should have been held, they held it on the second month. The people rejoiced so much in the spiritual healing that occurred that they all agreed to keep the Passover for an additional seven days, for a total of two weeks.[3]
- Under King Josiah after he had cleased the land of idols, and the book of the Law was found in the temple and read to the people: "Surely there was not holden such a passover from the days of the judges that judged Israel, nor in all the days of the kings of Israel, nor of the kings of Judah."[4]
- Following the completion of the second temple built after the return of the Jews from Babylon.[5]
- With Jesus and His Apostles.[6]
- Ezekiel's vision of a future Passover held following the building and dedication of the latter-day temple in Jerusalem.[7]

1 Numbers 9:4.
2 Joshua 5:3–12.
3 2 Chronicles 30.
4 2 Kings 23:22; 2 Chronicles 35.
5 Ezra 6:15–20.
6 Mattthew 26:2, 17–19; Luke 22; John 13–14.
7 Ezekiel 45:21.

CHAPTER 16

The Feast of Unleavened Bread—*Hag HaMatzot*

Seven days shall ye eat unleavened bread;
even the first day ye shall put away leaven out of your houses:
for whosoever eateth leavened bread
from the first day until the seventh day,
that soul shall be cut off from Israel.
And in the first day there shall be an holy convocation,
and in the seventh day
here shall be an holy convocation to you;
no manner of work shall be done in them,
save that which every man must eat,
that only may be done of you.
And ye shall observe the feast of unleavened
bread; for in this selfsame day
have I brought your armies out of the land of Egypt:
therefore shall ye observe this day
in your generations by an ordinance for ever.
In the first month, on the fourteenth day of the month at even,
ye shall eat unleavened bread,
until the one and twentieth day of the month at even.
Seven days shall there be no leaven found in your houses:
for whosoever eateth that which is leavened,
even that soul shall be cut off from the congregation of Israel,
whether he be a stranger, or born in the land.[1]

The Feast of Unleavened Bread begins on the 15th of Nisan, and lasts for seven days. It is now celebrated with the Passover, and has been discussed throughout the previous chapters.

---

1 Exodus 12:15–19.

CHAPTER 17

⸻ ❦ ⸻

Passover and Feast of Unleavened Bread Work Chart

Whosoever drinketh of the water that I shall give him shall never thirst;
but the water that I shall give him shall be in him
a well of water springing up into everlasting life.[1]

WHILE WE HAVE DISCUSSED A NUMBER OF POSSIBLE MEANINGS and applications for the various symbols and rituals of the spring feasts, there will be more that present themselves to you, personally. Each time you read the scriptures, partake of the sacrament, or attend the temple, new inspiration may come to you for application needed at that time. In this way, we realize the Savior's promise of living water springing fresh within us as we come to Him with the desire to see, know, understand, and apply.

The following chart is a personal work chart for you. The symbols of Passover and the Feast of Unleavened Bread are listed in the first column. A specific application to Christ for each is listed in the second column. The third column is for personal insight and application. There may be one application to the Savior listed, and one idea for personal insight, but I invite you to write within the empty spaces—and all over the page, or in a journal—the insights that are coming to you today.

Passover—14th Nisan and Feast of Unleavened Bread—15th Nisan (7 days)

Symbol	Christ	Personal Insight/ Application
Lamb	Lamb of God	
Chosen 10th day	Entered Jerusalem on the 10th	
Sacrificed 14th day	Jesus sacrificed on the 14th of Nisan	
Whole assembly gathered to "consent"— one lamb per family	Whole assembly "consented" to Jesus's death	Jesus died for each family and each individual—personally
Blood on doorposts	Christ's atoning blood saves and delivers	Is Christ's blood on the "doorposts" of my heart?
No bone broken	Not a bone of His body was broken	

Symbol	Christ	Personal Insight/ Application
Must eat all	Performed the Atonement fully— no "halfway"	I must fully partake of the Atonement of Christ—no holding back
Eaten with bitter herbs	Christ partook of the "bitter cup"	
Eaten with fresh herbs	Christ offers hope of eternal life	
Eaten with unleaven bread—sin removed; special process of preparation and baking	Christ was beaten with stripes, bruised, crushed, pierced, broken to remove sin from mankind	
4 cups of wine with symbolic nature: • "I will bring you out" • "I will deliver you" • "I will redeem you" • "I will take you to me"	• Christ "brings us out of the wilderness of sin/the world" • He "delivers us" from the bondage of sin and spiritual death" • He "redeems us" through His blood and atonement • He "takes us to Him" in His Kingdom with the Father	
The Afikomen, hidden dessert: • three matzahs • middle broken • one piece hidden for children to find	• Three members of the Godhead • Christ is broken • When one "finds" Christ, he must "become as a child"	

Symbol	Christ	Personal Insight/ Application
The Hallel sung (Psalm 118)	Many images and prophecies of Christ in this song	"Jehovah saves . . . Jehovah save me now."
A new year	Christ offers hope of a new life	

---

1 John 4:14.

CHAPTER 18

~~~~~~~~~~~~~~~~

The Feast of Firstfruits and The Savior: "The Firstfruits of Them Who Slept"

But now is Christ risen from the dead,
and become the first fruits of them that slept.
For since by man came death,
by man came also the resurrection of the dead.
For as in Adam all die, even so in Christ shall all be made alive.[1]

ON THE FIRST DAY OF PASSOVER, PRIESTS WERE TO SELECT THE choicest barley grain to be used in the Firstfruits ritual from a naturally irrigated field near the temple. According to tradition, on the evening of the next day, three threshers were to go to the previously selected field, each with a sickle and basket. They were to ask the following questions three times of bystanders: "Has the sun gone down?" "With this sickle?" "Into this basket?" "On this Sabbath?"—and lastly, "Shall I reap?" After being answered in the affirmative, their baskets were filled and taken back to the temple, where the grain was thrashed with canes, and ground in a barley mill till it was considered to be sufficiently fine to be offered. It was mixed heavily with olive oil and a handful of frankincense, and then "waved" before the altar of the Lord.[2]

As with all of the other rituals of the feast and festival days, those associated with the Feast of Firstfruits have noticeable application to the events of the Messiah's Atonement, death, and resurrection.

The grain was to be selected and noted the first day of Passover— the temple priests planned that Jesus should be cut down and sacrificed; they arrested Him on the "first day" of Passover, the night He performed the Atonement in the Garden of Gethsemane.[3]

Three "thrashers" were to ask bystanders three questions to determine that they were selecting the correct grain, and that it was taken according to specific guidelines, then mixed with oil and frankincense—Three apostles witnessed Jesus's Atonement in the Garden of Gethsemane. On the "2nd day" of Passover,[4] Jesus was taken down from the cross just as the sun was setting, beginning a new Sabbath day. He was "cut down" from the land of the living; taken from the Father's field, and nearby His "house," the temple. Jesus is the Firstfruit of the Father; the Firstborn. He was thrashed with rods (canes) and whips, and had been "ground" down finely at the mill of Gethsemane. In addition, He was the "choicest" offering—the "finest" of all the sacrifices ever presented to the Father. His blood, in the olive press of the Garden, oozed out in agony (Gethsemane means "olive press"). When He was buried, oil and frankincense were used to anoint His body.

A Christmas song states that "the world in solemn stillness lay" at the time of Christ's birth.[5] This sentiment is perhaps even more appropriate in describing the space of time when Jesus lay in the tomb. In Jerusalem, His burial came with the Sabbath eve: a time when activity ceased, and movements were curtailed. In the new world, the Nephites lay in fear and trembling, as darkness covered them, and "for the space of three days there was no light seen."[6] Earthquakes, storms and upheavals had devastated their cities at the time of the Savior's death. They heard His voice speak to them in the midst of the darkness and terror, identifying Himself as "Jesus Christ the Son of God."[7] Their astonishment over the events, together with the sound of His voice caused "silence in the land for the space of many hours."[8]

Perhaps there was no more reverent and "still" a place than on the other side of the veil, where "an innumerable company of the spirits of the just" were "awaiting the advent of the Son of God into the spirit world." While those on earth mourned over the events that had just transpired, this group of faithful saints "were filled with joy and gladness, and were rejoicing together because the day of their deliverance was at hand." They "had looked upon the long absence of their spirits from their bodies as a bondage," and eagerly looked forward to the Savior's completion of His mission, when He would at last fulfill the promise of atonement and resurrection—not only for Himself—"the firstfruits of them who slept"—but for all of mankind. Unlike the many who had rejected Him in mortality, these "bowed the knee and acknowledged the Son of God as their Redeemer and Deliverer from death and the chains of hell. Their countenances shone, and the radiance from the presence of the Lord rested upon them, and they sang praises unto his holy name."[9]

While His body lay in the tomb, Jesus not only spoke to the Nephites, but He also went to "declare liberty to the captives [in the Spirit World] who had been faithful . . . and preached to them the everlasting gospel."[10] His character and personality are beautifully portrayed by the nature of His interaction with both groups. Generous and magnanimous, Jesus displayed no bitterness, hurt feelings, or grudge-bearing in His manner; there was no "tallying" of the wrongs done to Him by those whom He had come to save.

Jesus urged the Nephites: " . . . will ye not now return unto me, and repent of your sins, and be converted, that I may heal you? Yea, verily I say unto you, if ye will come unto me ye shall have eternal life. Behold, mine arm of mercy is extended towards you, and whomsoever will come, him will I receive."[11]

As He spoke to the Nephites, Jesus did not number the wrongs so recently perpetrated against Him, but He did express His sorrow over those who had been lost, and had turned away from Him: "O ye people of these great cities which have fallen, who are descendants of Jacob, yea, who are of the house of Israel, how oft have I gathered you as a hen gathereth her chickens under her wings, and have nourished you. And again, how oft would I have gathered you as a hen gathereth her chickens under her wings, yea, O ye people of the house of Israel, who have fallen; yea, O ye people of the house of Israel, ye that dwell at Jerusalem, as ye that have fallen; yea, how oft would I have gathered you as a hen gathereth her chickens, and ye would not."[12]

His sacrifice was given willingly and with love; His sorrow comes when it is not accepted.

In Jerusalem, those that loved Him waited in fear and mourning. The women waited for the Sabbath to end, so that they might go and finish their loving ministrations in preparing His body for burial. The disciples kept themselves in a room with the doors shut "for fear of the Jews."[13] The chief priests and Pharisees arranged to have the tomb sealed with a stone, and soldiers set to watch; for they feared that Jesus's disciples would come and take His body, "Saying, Sir, we remember that that deceiver said, while he was yet alive, After three days I will rise again. Command therefore that the sepulcher be made sure until the third day, lest his disciples come by night, and steal him away, and say unto the people, He is risen from the dead:"[14]

The desperate efforts of the priests and the soldiers could not restrain the Lord Jehovah from exiting the tomb at the very moment He desired! Early Sunday morning, two angels appeared and rolled away the stone that covered the opening to the grave. An earthquake accompanied their act. Did the earthquake occur in conjunction with the Resurrection itself? The guards shook with fear and shock, but later, recovered their "natural man"[15] equanimity in order to accept money from the priests to lie and say that the disciples had stolen Jesus's body.[16] Although *their* witness would not be given, there *would be many others* willing to testify that Jesus lived again.

The first witnesses of Christ's resurrection were women. Elder Bruce R. McConkie wrote:

> How much there is incident to the death, burial, and resurrection of our Lord which ennobles and exalts faithful women. They wept at the cross, sought to care for his wounded and lifeless body, and came to his tomb to weep and worship for their friend and Master. And so it is not strange that we find a woman, Mary of Magdala, chosen and singled out from all the disciples, even including the apostles, to be the first mortal to see and bow in the presence of a resurrected being. Mary, who had been healed of much and who loved much, saw the risen Christ![17]

We sense that Mary and the other women had spent a restless Sabbath. While it was "yet dark,"[18] the women made their way to the sepulcher, precious spices in their hands. As they walked, they wondered how they might remove the stone that had been placed over the entrance of the tomb, "for it was very great."[19] But when they arrived at their destination, they found neither the guards nor the body of their beloved Messiah. The two angels who had earlier frightened the soldiers lingered at the sacred site, sitting, in fact, on the very stone that was intended to block the way of any intruders.[20] The women were frightened, but the angels reassured them:

Be not affrighted: Ye seek Jesus of Nazareth, who was crucified . . .
Why seek ye the living among the dead?
He is not here, but is risen:
remember how he spake unto you
when he was yet in Galilee,
Saying the Son of Man must be delivered
into the hands of sinful men,
and be crucified, and the third day rise again . . .
go your way, tell his disciples and Peter
that he goeth before you into Galilee
there shall ye see him, as he said unto you.[21]

Mary's news caused an immediate response from both Peter and John: they *ran* to the tomb to see for themselves. There is sweetness in the details; John, the younger, outran Peter, but waited respectfully outside of the burial place for Peter to enter first. Perhaps it was his sense of reverence for what had occurred there, or perhaps it was due to the fact that the Lord had decreed that Peter was to be their leader, and John was already showing his acquiescence. They found the grave clothes, with the head cloth wrapped and folded apart from the rest lying on the stone, evidence that this was no hurried theft of the body. John wrote that although they did not "yet [know] the scripture that he must rise again from the dead," he yet "believed" when he saw this evidence.[22] Peter "wondered in himself at that which [had] come to pass" as he made his way back to the others.[23] The women's stories seemed like "idle tales" to the remainder of the apostles, and they did not believe them.[24] Afterwards, Jesus "upbraided them" for "their unbelief and hardness of heart."[25]

As Mary lingered near the holy place, a Man she thought to be a gardener came near. "Woman, why weepest thou? Whom seekest thou?" He asked. Pathetically, she implored: "Sir if thou have borne him hence, tell me where thou hast laid him, and I will take him away." Such was her love, that without aid of another, she would attempt to carry His body by herself. He answered with one word: "Mary." At the sound of her name, spoken by the beloved voice, she joyfully cried out: "Rabboni," or "Master." She could not refrain from embracing Him, but He counseled, "Hold me not; for I am not ascended to my Father . . ."[26]

Elder Bruce R. McConkie explained:

We cannot believe that the caution which withheld from Jesus the embrace of Mary was anything more than the building of a proper wall of reserve between intimates who are now on two sides of the veil. If a resurrected brother appeared to a mortal brother, or a resurrected husband appeared to a mortal wife, would they be free to embrace each other on the same terms of intimacy as had prevailed when both were mortals? But perhaps there was more in Jesus's statement than Mary related or than John recorded, for in a very short time we shall see a group of faithful women hold Jesus by his feet as they worship him.[27]

The Lord's first appearance was to Mary Magdalene. Later, a group of faithful women saw Him, then two discouraged disciples who were walking along the road to Emmaus.[28] At last, He appeared to ten of the apostles (Thomas was absent), had them touch His wounds, and ate with them.[29] He would make another appearance to the apostles eight days later, and would show Himself to more than five hundred at once in Galilee.[30] At some point, there was a private meeting with Peter,[31] and with His own half-brother, James, formerly a non-believer.[32] After His ascension, He appeared in physical form to the Nephites,[33] to Paul,[34] and to others, including Joseph Smith in the present era.[35]

In each appearance, our Savior invites all to see for themselves; to touch the wounds in His hands and feet, and to thrust their hands into His side. Elder Jeffrey R. Holland taught:

In fact, in a resurrected, otherwise perfected body, our Lord . . . has chosen to retain for the benefit of his disciples the wounds in his hands and his feet and his side—signs, if you will, that painful things happen even to the pure and perfect. Signs, if you will, that pain in this world is *not* evidence that God doesn't love you. It is the *wounded* Christ who is the captain of our soul—he who yet bears the scars of sacrifice, the lesions of love and humility and forgiveness. Those wounds are what he invites young and old, then and now, to step forward and see and feel.[36]

Thomas had told the others that he would not believe until he could see and feel for himself. The Savior chastened him: "Thomas, because thou hast seen me, thou hast believed: blessed are they that have not seen, and yet have believed."[37]

We, too, can have a witness of Christ's resurrection from the dead. President Howard W. Hunter urged:

> It is the responsibility and joy of all men and women everywhere to "seek this Jesus of whom the prophets and apostles have [testified]" and to have the spiritual witness of His divinity. *It is the right and blessing of all who humbly seek, to hear the voice of the Holy Spirit, bearing witness of the Father and His resurrected Son.*[38]

Anciently, the firstfruit offering was to be waved before the temple altar on the day following the Sabbath. Saturday was the Sabbath, and Jesus rose from the grave on Sunday morning—the morning of the Firstfruits offering. Jesus is the "firstfruits of them that slept."[39] As the first sheaves of barley were being waved before the great temple altar and the people thanked God for the grain that provided their bread, Jesus, who is the Bread of Life, presented Himself to the Father in His heavenly temple.

---

1 1 Corinthians 15:20–22.

2 Edersheim, *The Temple: Its Ministry and Services*, 205.

3 John 11:47–57.

4 Don't be confused by the sundown-to-sundown manner in which a day was counted. There are not "two days of Passover," but I have referred to it in the context that can be understood by those who count a day as dawn to midnight.

5 "It Came Upon the Midnight Clear," *Hymns*, no. 207.

6 3 Nephi 8:23.

7 3 Nephi 9:15.

8 3 Nephi 10:1.

9 Doctrine and Covenants 138:12–50; see also 1 Peter 4:6.

10 Doctrine and Covenants 138:18–19, 27.

11 3 Nephi 9:13–14.

12 3 Nephi 10:4–5.

13 John 20:19.

14 Matthew 27:62–66, Joseph Smith Translation.

15 Mosiah 3:19.

16 Matthew 28:2–4, 11–14, Joseph Smith Translation.

17 McConkie, *Doctrinal New Testament Commentary*, 1:843.

18 John 20:1.

19 Mark 16:4.

20 Mark 16:4 Joseph Smith Translation.

21 Mark 16:6–8, Joseph Smith Translation; Luke 24:5–7.

22 John 20:3–9

23 Luke 24:12.

24 Mark 16:11; Luke 24:11.

25 Mark 16:14.

26 John 20:11–17.

27 McConkie, *Mortal Messiah*, 4:264.

28 Luke 24:13–24.

29 Luke 24:36–43.

30 1 Corinthians 15:6.

31 Luke 24:34.

32 1 Corinthians 15:7; James 1:5–6.

33 3 Nephi 11.

34 1 Corinthians 15:8.

35 Joseph Smith History 1:16–17.

36 Holland, "'This Do In Remembrance of Me,'" Oct. 1995 General Conference.

37 John 20:29.

38 Hunter, "He Is Risen," Apr. 1988 General Conference.

39 1 Corinthians 15:20; 2 Nephi 2:9.

—⁓⁑⁓—

CHAPTER 19

The Feast of Firstfruits and The Lord's Vineyard

And it came to pass that the Lord of the vineyard wept,
and said unto the servant:
What could I have done more for my vineyard?[1]

THE FEAST OF FIRSTFRUITS, OR *BIKKURIM*, IS OBSERVED IN CONnection with the Passover Feast and the week of Unleavened Bread. There is some question as to whether it was performed the day after the Passover or the day after the Sabbath (both were referred to as a Sabbath).[2] This festival is no longer observed in traditional Judaism today.[3]

The Israelites crossed the Red Sea on 17th Nisan, the day that later became known and celebrated as the Feast of Firstfruits. That crossing through the waters symbolized a baptism, as the Israelites were "born again" unto God as a nation. According to Jeremiah, "Israel was holiness unto the Lord, and the firstfruits of his increase."[4]

The Lord then "planted" the Israelites in the Promised Land, and looked for them to bring forth fruit unto Him. Prior to their arrival in their new lands, they were provided miraculous food in the wilderness. The last manna fell on Passover, before crossing into Canaan. From that point on, they were to eat from the labors of their own hands.[5]

Although they would no longer have manna and quail fall from heaven to feed them, it was important for the Israelites to acknowledge that all that they *did have* came through the bounty of God's blessings upon them. Accordingly, they were to offer up their first fruits of the land as a sacrifice unto the Lord. The firstling of the flock was also to be given to the Lord. In similar fashion, we offer up our tithes and offerings first, before paying for our other living expenses.

When we offer the first and the best of our harvest or increase unto the Lord, we recognize that all that we have comes from Him. We are simply returning something He has already given us in a token of gratitude and hope that with that obedient acknowledgment, He will continue to provide as He has done in the past. King Benjamin taught this principle to his people:

> *And behold, all that he requires of you*
> *is to keep his commandments;*
> *and he has promised you that if ye would keep his*
> *commandments ye should prosper in the land;*
> *and he never doth vary from that which he hath said;*
> *therefore, if ye do keep his commandments*
> *he doth bless you and prosper you.*
> *And now, in the first place,*
> *he hath created you, and granted unto you your lives,*
> *for which ye are indebted unto him.*
> *And secondly, he doth require that ye*
> *should do as he hath commanded you;*
> *for which if ye do, he doth immediately bless you;*
> *and therefore he hath paid you.*
> *And ye are still indebted unto him,*
> *and are, and will be, forever and ever;*
> *Therefore, of what have ye to boast?* [6]

All too often, we begin to take credit for the fruits of our labors, feel that we have earned what we have by our own hard work, and that our harvest belongs entirely to ourselves. King Benjamin also addressed this attitude:

> *And now I ask, can ye say aught of yourselves?*
> *I answer you, Nay.*
> *Ye cannot say that ye are even as much as the dust of the earth;*
> *yet ye were created of the dust of the earth;*
> *but behold, it belongeth to him who created you.* [7]

Being *fruitful* is not just about offering the first of our harvest, or increase, to the Lord. It is also about *stewardship*. What are we doing with the gifts the Lord has put into our hands? Even the Garden of Eden required work: the Lord told Adam and Eve that they were to "dress" and "keep" the Garden.[8] Are we cultivating—*working*—the "land" the Lord has given us for an inheritance? This includes not just the earth (though that is certainly required of our stewardship), but also our homes, our tabernacle-bodies, our time and talents, and all that the Lord has given us.

> . . . *for it is required of the Lord,*
> *at the hand of every steward,*
> *to render an account of his stewardship,*
> *both in time and in eternity.*
> *For he who is faithful and wise in time*
> *is accounted worthy to inherit*
> *the mansions prepared for him of my Father.*[9]

Jeremiah recorded the Lord's frustration with the early Israelites: "And I brought you into a plentiful country, to eat the fruit thereof and the goodness thereof; but when ye entered, ye defiled my land, and made mine heritage an abomination."[10]

What is the spiritual underpinning of this accusation? Surely the Lord is not simply speaking of farming a plot of earth. The early Israelites "defiled" the land by what they allowed to enter their hearts, and what their thoughts were centered on instead of the sacred stewardship the Lord had provided them with—to be separate, or *set apart*, holy, and distinct from their neighbors, as they built a kingdom of holiness.

Isaiah 5 and Jacob 5 both tell the story of the Lord's efforts to help His people to bring forth good fruit. Isaiah explains that the Lord planted His people "in a very fruitful hill" and "looked that it should bring forth grapes, [but] it brought forth wild grapes."[11]

> *For the vineyard of the Lord of hosts is the house of Israel,*
> *and the men of Judah his pleasant plant:*
> *and he looked for judgment* [justice], *but behold oppression;*
> *for righteousness, but behold a cry* [riotous or raucous outcry].[12]

Unfortunately, the people He planted in both the Old and New Worlds struggled to bring forth good fruit, and failed to acknowledge the Lord as their Master.

And it came to pass that the Lord of the vineyard wept,
and said unto the servant:
What could I have done more for my vineyard? [13]

As children of God, we often fail to recognize His role as the Lord of the vineyard. We resist becoming His firstfruits people. We resist Him planting us where we may not want to be, and we rebel against His efforts to prune us, or to dig around our roots. We think we know what is best for our lives, and when we become proud, we fail to submit to His ministrations. In that pride, we are tempted to withhold acknowledgment of the Lord's goodness, and resent giving the firstfruits of our labor back to Him.

Adam and Eve were commanded to offer the firstlings of their flock to God, as it was "a similitude of the sacrifice of the Only Begotten of the Father."[14] Cain offered an offering unto the Lord of "fruit of the ground" and resented the fact that God would not accept it.[15] It was not just that Cain did not offer the proper offering, but more, that Cain was motivated by Satan's mocking whisper to give the offering.[16] Cain's resentment and envy led to the murder of his brother, Abel. Cain's first step in that direction really began with Cain's earliest recorded remark of, "Who is the Lord that I should know him?"[17] Cain had a spirit of rebellion that prevented him from seeing God's true nature and role as loving Father, and he submitted himself to Satan rather than to the Lord.

Our offerings represent our recognition and gratitude for all that the Lord has given us. When they are given with an understanding heart, we hope that we, ourselves, are also "fruitful" to God. It's not just the labor of our hands that we want to offer, but our whole selves, entirely. The firstborn male lambs required in early sacrifices foreshadowed the fact that the Father and His Son, Jesus Christ, *would—and did*—offer up their very best in our behalf. How can we give any less than our best in return?

A Primary song teaches:

How could the Father tell the world of sacrifice, of death?

He sent His Son to die for us and rise with living breath.
What does the Father ask of us? What do the scriptures say?
Have faith, have hope, live like His Son, help others on their way.
What does he ask? Live like his Son.[18]

The Lord tried to teach His people about the progressive nature of sacrifice: that it moved from an outward counting of fruit, to an inward state of the heart, to a forward-looking way of being holy and set apart that pertained to generations to come. After they left Egypt, the Lord commanded the Israelites: "the firstborn of thy sons shalt thou give unto me,"[19] in remembrance of the fact that He had obtained their freedom through the sacrifice of the Egyptians' firstborn sons, but more, that He had obtained their salvation through the sacrifice of *His* Firstborn Son. Of course, God was not asking the Israelites to kill their sons, but He *was* asking them to raise their children up unto Him, and to understand the covenant of holiness. They were to be "a kingdom of priests, and an holy nation."[20] The Lord praised Abraham for this centuries earlier, when he said: "For I know him, that he will command his children and his household after him, and they shall keep the way of the Lord."[21]

When Hannah offered her firstborn son, Samuel, to the Lord, she recognized that she was not *losing* her son by this sacrifice. In her words, she had *lent* Samuel to the Lord.[22] As a popular sentiment states, *He* has actually lent our children to *us*. They are *His*, created spiritually by Him before they came to inhabit mortal bodies we helped to create for them. He has entrusted them to our care, with the hope that we will teach them of their true relationship to Him and to the Savior, Jesus Christ. When we understand this, we begin to truly understand our own relationship to God, and what offering our hearts unto Him really means. Fruit and animals are simply stepping-stones to help us gain that understanding.

Children are frequently referred to as *the fruit of our loins*. We are promised that that particular fruit is eternal when we are true to our covenants. Hannah knew that while she had lent her son, Samuel, to the Lord during his lifetime, she could look forward with joy to being with him eternally. Because of her selfless offering, Samuel became a prophet, anointed King David, and aided in David's unification of

Israel under God. With the combined vision of David and Samuel, Israel began to see what it meant to be a holy nation.

The Lord's command to give one's firstborn son to Him was amended when He called the tribe of Levi to officiate in the tabernacle and temple. He said: "I have taken the Levites from among the children of Israel instead of all the firstborn . . . among the children of Israel: therefore the Levites shall be mine; Because all the firstborn are mine; for on the day that I smote all the firstborn in the land of Egypt I hallowed unto me all the firstborn in Israel, both man and beast: mine shall they be: I am the Lord."[23]

The *setting apart* of the Levites, or the firstborn, should aid us in having a new perspective for baby blessings and ordinations, as well as our own opportunity to be *set apart* to serve in the Church. What did it mean for Samuel to be *set apart*, or for a Levite to be *set apart*? Ronald D. Maines explained,

> In our dispensation, we again enjoy the blessings accompanying this ordinance [of setting apart]. As a priesthood ordinance, the action of setting an individual apart involves divine power, promise, and holiness. It is a special event which may be accompanied by an outpouring of the Spirit. As with other gospel ordinances, the inspiration attending this ordinance may deepen our understanding, elevate our spirits, remind us of our possibilities, and motivate us to a higher, richer quality of life.
>
> We receive an investiture of authority from the Lord when we are set apart. We can thereafter act as the Lord's authorized agents and carry out his errands with his approval . . .
>
> When we are set apart, we also receive the right to obtain knowledge and revelation to accomplish our assigned tasks. . . .
>
> We also have the right to receive special strength of body and spirit. As we seek this strength, we must also gird ourselves for the work. Having been set apart for the work of the Lord, we must, in a manner of speaking, set ourselves apart from the world to the work of the Lord's kingdom. By being set apart, we promise to consecrate a portion of our time and talents to magnify our callings.[24]

We are the Lord's vineyard. He is looking for us to bring forth fruit in a bountiful harvest. Do we recognize Him as the Master of the Vineyard?

Do we allow Him to plant us where He will, and to cultivate, prune, and dig around our roots? Do we look for ways to magnify our own stewardship in assisting Him in the work of the vineyard? How are we using the gifts He has given us? Are we teaching the younger generation what it means to be a holy nation, and a kingdom of priests (and priestesses?). Are we offering up our all unto God?

1 Jacob 5:41.

2 Exodus 23:17–19; Leviticus 23:9–11; see Edersheim, *The Temple: Its Ministry and Services*, 203.

3 Chumney, *The Seven Festivals of the Messiah*, 12.

4 Jeremiah 2:3.

5 See Joshua 5:10–12.

6 Mosiah 2:22–24.

7 Mosiah 2:25.

8 Genesis 2:15.

9 Doctrine and Covenants 72:3–4.

10 Jeremiah 2:7.

11 Isaiah 5:2.

12 Isaiah 5:7.

13 Jacob 5:41.

14 Moses 5:7.

15 See Moses 5:19, 21.

16 Moses 5:18.

17 Moses 5:16.

18 "He Sent His Son," *Children's Songbook*, 34–35.

19 Exodus 22:29.

20 Exodus 19:5–6.

21 Genesis 18:19.

22 1 Samuel 1:28.

23 Numbers 3:12–13.

24 Maines, "What exactly does it mean when we are 'set apart' for a Church calling?" Feb. 1992 *Ensign.*

CHAPTER 20

Feast of Firstfruits,
Bikkurim, Work Chart

THERE IS MUCH TO PONDER IN CONNECTION TO THE FEAST OF Firstfruits or *Bikkurim*. Most important is the fulfillment of the symbols and rituals in the life, mission, death, and resurrection of Jesus Christ. He is the Firstfruits of the Father, and through Him, we obtain life. His life, love, and Atonement are represented in the fruit of the tree—and the tree itself—in Lehi's vision.[1]

Jesus Christ is also the Master of the vineyard. He has planted His people in various locations, and He is looking for us to produce fruit. In order to do so, we must respond to His ministrations in our behalf, as he "digs, prunes," and works with us.[2]

The following work chart is an opportunity for you to ponder the symbols of the Feast of Firstfruits, and discover personal applications to your own life.

How will what you have learned affect your offerings to God?

How will it affect your gratitude and appreciate for the Atonement of Jesus Christ?

How will you continue to "bear fruit" throughout your life?

FEAST OF FIRSTFRUITS, BIKKURIM—17TH NISAN

Symbol	Christ	Personal Insight/ Application
First of the spring grain	Jesus is the first creation of the Father; He is the Bread of Life; He is the "firstfruits of them that slept"	
Israelites—Red Sea—17th Nisan; Born unto God as the first nation of Israel		
Israel/Nephite Vineyard Challenges		
Grain to be chosen first day of Passover	Priests determined to put Jesus to death on the first day of Passover	
Grain from naturally irrigated field nearby temple	Jesus is the Living Water; He performed the Atonement nearby the temple	
Three threshers to witness which grain to be harvested: "Has the sun gone down?" "Shall I reap?"	Three apostles witnessed the atonement in Gethsemane—Christ was "cut down" from life	

Symbol	Christ	Personal Insight/ Application
Grain thrashed with canes and ground in mill	Jesus thrashed with canes (rods) and whips, ground and pressed down in "olive press" (Gethsemane)	
Flour mixed with olive oil and frankincense	Christ's blood oozed like the oil from the press; the olive oil is used for anointing and healing. His lifeless body was anointed with frankincense	
The offering waved before the altar	Christ was presented before the altar of His Father	

---

1 See 1 Nephi 11.
2 See Jacob 5.

CHAPTER 21

Feast of Pentecost, *Shavuot*

*And ye shall count unto you from the morrow after the
sabbath, from the day that ye brought the sheaf of the wave
offering; seven sabbaths shall be complete: Even unto the morrow
after the seventh sabbath shall ye number fifty days;
and ye shall offer a new meat offering unto the Lord.*

*Ye shall bring out of your habitations
two wave loaves of two tenth deals:
they shall be of fine flour; they shall be baken with leaven;
they are the firstfruits unto the Lord.*

*And ye shall offer with the bread
seven lambs without blemish of the first year,
and one young bullock, and two rams:
they shall be for a burnt offering unto the Lord,
with their meat offering, and their drink offerings,
even an offering made by fire, of sweet savour unto the Lord.*

*Then ye shall sacrifice one kid
of the goats for a sin offering,
and two lambs of the first year
for a sacrifice of peace offerings.*

*And the priest shall wave them
with the bread of the firstfruits for a wave offering
before the Lord, with the two lambs:
they shall be holy to the Lord for the priest.*

*And ye shall proclaim on the selfsame day,
that it may be an holy convocation unto you:*

ye shall do no servile work therein:
it shall be a statute for ever in all your dwellings
throughout your generations.[1]

THE FEAST OF PENTECOST, ALSO CALLED THE FEAST OF WEEKS, or *Shavuot,* is marked by counting fifty days (*pente*) from the Sabbath following Passover, or seven weeks following the Firstfruits offering of barley. This counting period is known as the *counting of the omer.*[2]

Pentecost, or *Shavuot,* is sometimes viewed as the culmination of the Passover season, which makes sense if we think of the purposeful journey of the Israelites from Egypt at Passover to Mt. Sinai for their meeting with Jehovah fifty days later. Escape from Egypt and "baptism" in the Red Sea were simply the first steps necessary to the all-important destination, where Jehovah would renew the Abrahamic covenant with his posterity. Pentecost celebrates that event.

Later, as He revealed instructions regarding the building of the tabernacle and its services, the Lord included the requirements as to how to keep the Feast of Pentecost. While the Feast of Firstfruits celebrated the barley harvest, the Feast of Pentecost became associated with the wheat harvest, and is also sometimes referred to as a "feast of firstfruits," as two loaves of finely ground wheat bread (with leaven) are waved before the temple altar as a sacrifice. One was not to eat any wheat from the harvest until the first offerings were presented before the Lord.

It is most interesting that the two loaves of bread (approximately five pounds each) were to contain leaven. Leaven, as we have seen, was strictly prohibited in the previous celebration of Passover and the Feast of Unleavened Bread. Leaven was never to touch the altar. Yet, these two loaves were "waved" in front of the altar in acknowledgment and gratitude for the bounty of the new harvest.

Many are puzzled by the fact that the two loaves were specifically to contain leaven. Some have concluded that the leaven acknowledges a "sinful" people presenting themselves to the Lord, but what is the meaning behind presenting *two* loaves? Could the two loaves represent the House of Israel and the Gentiles? Israel was already considered the "firstfruit" unto God, and at a later Pentecost celebration, Gentiles would also join the family of faith and covenant, becoming adopted members of Israel.[3] We shall see other aspects of the Feast that also seem to foreshadow the adoption of the Gentiles into Israel, but we do not have any definitive answers to the two-loaves ritual, or the animal sacrifices associated with this Feast. The two loaves are offered along with seven lambs, one young bullock, two rams, and a goat.[4] Two lambs are offered separately with the loaves as a "peace offering."

The offering of the two loaves and two lambs was unique in character in that it was "waved" in front of the altar—the loaves together with the two living lambs before sacrifice, and then again following the sacrifice of the lambs.[5]

Of special note is the fact that the Book of Ruth is included in every *Shavuot* reading. This may be another foreshadowing of the adoption of the Gentiles into Israel.

We first meet Ruth when she is living with her widowed mother-in-law, Naomi, in Moab. Naomi and her husband had gone to Moab during a famine in Israel, and Naomi's two sons had married Moabite women during their sojourn there. But, when all of the men had died, Naomi determined to go back home to Bethlehem. She encouraged her two daughters-in-law to return to the home of their parents, but Ruth would not leave Naomi. She said:

> *Entreat me not to leave thee, or to return from following after thee:*
> *for whither thou goest, I will go;*
> *and where thou lodgest, I will lodge:*
> *thy people shall be my people, and thy God my God:*[6]

Ruth and Naomi arrived in Bethlehem "in the beginning of barley harvest"[7] (which we now recognize as Passover season, and the time of the Feast of Firstfruits). Ruth went out into the fields of the harvest to glean what was left after the reapers. The field belonged to Boaz, a kinsman of Naomi, and Boaz was impressed by Ruth's loving care of Naomi.[8] He gave instructions for the reapers to purposefully leave more of the grain behind for Ruth, and by threshing time, Boaz determined to marry Ruth and to redeem her from poverty and widowhood. From their posterity came King David and Jesus Christ.[9]

While today, many Jews stay up all night on *Shavuot* (Pentecost) reading the Torah, the book of Ruth is the only book that is always read in full. Ruth, a Gentile, was adopted into the family of Israel, and the Savior was born through her lineage.

It may be that the definitive meaning for each of the offerings, sacrifices and rituals of Pentecost is obscured for us because the offerings and sacrifices are overshadowed by the main celebratory focus of the Feast: the reception of the Law at Mt. Sinai for the Israelites, and later, the reception of the Holy Ghost for the early Christians.

---

1 Leviticus 23:15–21.
2 See Chumney, *The Seven Festivals of the Messiah*, 69–70.
3 Acts 2, 10.
4 See Leviticus 23:16–21; Numbers 28:26–31.
5 See Edersheim, *The Temple: Its Ministry and Services*, 210.
6 Ruth 1:16.
7 Ruth 1:22.
8 Ruth 2:11.
9 See Ruth 3–4.

CHAPTER 22

―――⁓∽⁓―――

Feast of Pentecost, *Shavuot:*
The Gift of the Law

And he said unto Abram,
Know of a surety that thy seed shall be a stranger
in a land that is not theirs,
and shall serve them;
and they shall afflict them four hundred years;
And also that nation, whom they shall serve, will I judge:
and afterward shall they come out with great substance. . . .
But in the fourth generation they shall come hither again.[1]

THE LORD PROMISED ABRAHAM THAT FOLLOWING 400 YEARS OF servitude in Egypt, his posterity would be brought forth again into the Promised Land, and have the opportunity to enter into The New and Everlasting Covenant as individuals and as a family.[2] Moses was called as the great prophet to deliver the children of Israel according to the promise. With the first Passover, Pharaoh consented to allow the Israelites to leave Egypt, and Moses led them to Mount Sinai, according to the prearrangements of the Lord.

When Moses and the children of Israel arrived at Sinai, the Lord instructed the people to take three days to ready themselves to meet Him, and prepare themselves to enter into a covenant with Him.[3] This event, intended to be an official binding covenantal relationship between Jehovah and His people, took place fifty days after Passover (or the Feast of Firstfruits). *Shavuot,* the Feast of Weeks, or Pentecost, is a commemoration of this event, and the giving of the Law of Jehovah to His people.

The Law, as it is referred to in these passages, is much more than the Law of Moses, as we shall see. It is the fulness of the Gospel of Jehovah-Christ, including every word that would be spoken by Him or His servants. The tie between His Law and the covenant were expressed in Jehovah's invitation to Israel on *Shavuot*:

> *Now therefore, if ye will obey my voice indeed,*
> *and keep my covenant,*
> *then ye shall be a peculiar treasure unto me above all people . . .*[4]

For the Jews (the only remaining people to clearly identify themselves as former Israel), *the Law* is the Torah, or the five books of Moses. The *Tanakh* includes the prophets and writings that Christians refer to as the *Old Testament*.

In about 600 BC, the Lord commanded that Nephi and his brothers should return to Jerusalem to obtain the plates of brass from Laban.[5] The plates contained "the Law," and the prophecies of the major prophets through Jeremiah.[6] Both Nephi and Lehi testified that these were necessary so that the Nephites could preserve the commandments of the Lord for their children.[7] The love of the Law, and their adherence to it, caused Lehi and his family to view themselves as a covenant people, the covenant family of Israel.

It's interesting to note that Nephi called to remembrance the miracles performed at Passover, when Moses delivered the Israelites, in order to convince his brothers to move forward with their mission.[8] Did the remembrance of the Passover miracle, and the first Pentecost, or *Shavuot*, influence Nephi's commitment to get the records at any cost?

The website *Judaism 101* explains:

> The period from Passover to *Shavu'ot* is a time of great anticipation. We count each of the days from the second day of Passover to the day before *Shavu'ot*, 49 days or 7 full weeks, hence the name of the festival. The counting reminds us of the important connection between Passover and *Shavu'ot*: Passover freed us physically from bondage, but the giving of the Torah on *Shavu'ot* redeemed us spiritually from our bondage to idolatry and immorality. *Shavu'ot* is also known as Pentecost, because it falls on the 50th day . . .
>
> It is noteworthy that the holiday is called the time of the *giving* of the Torah, rather than the time of the *receiving* of the Torah. The

sages point out that we are constantly in the process of receiving the Torah, that we receive it every day, but it was first given at this time. Thus it is the giving, not the receiving, that makes this holiday significant.[9]

The Day of Pentecost (*Shavout*) as recorded in Acts 2 has many similarities to the events that happened at Mt. Sinai. The mountain at Sinai was filled with "smoke" or glory, and the Lord "descended upon it in fire,"[10] while the room at Pentecost was filled with cloven tongues of fire.[11] A trumpet called to the people on the mount, while a sound from heaven filled the upper room.[12] All that was done on Mt. Sinai was done "in the sight of all the people;"[13] what happened in the upper room in Jerusalem expanded outwardly until the sounds from heaven attracted all the people in the city.[14] Most wonderful of all is the fact that while 3,000 people died over the golden calf incident at Sinai, 3,000 people accepted Christ and were baptized on the Day of Pentecost.[15]

Jehovah, Jesus Christ, was able to give His Law, or covenant, to the early Christian apostles and their followers, and have it accepted—for a time—until, with the Apostasy, it was lost again.

The blessings of Pentecost or *Shavuot* were restored again in our dispensation. Joseph Smith said of the events surrounding the dedication of the Kirtland Temple:

> It was a Pentecost and an endowment indeed, long to be remembered, for the sound shall go forth from this place into all the world, and the occurrences of this day shall be handed down upon the pages of sacred history to all generations; as the day of Pentecost, so shall this day be numbered and celebrated as a year of jubilee, and time of rejoicing to the Saints of the Most High God.[16]

At the temple dedication, many people reported that they saw angels walking on top of the temple, saw light resembling fire, and heard sounds like a rushing wind.[17] Moses came to the temple and committed the keys of the gathering of Israel. Elias, also appeared with the dispensation of the gospel of Abraham (including the Abrahamic covenant), and Elijah came in fulfillment of the Malachi promise and prophecy.[18] Most glorious of all, the Savior, Himself appeared, establishing His Law and covenant with the saints of the latter-days.

His eyes were as a flame of fire;
the hair of his head was white like pure snow;
his countenance shone above the brightness of the sun;
and his voice was as the sound of the rushing of great waters,
even the voice of Jehovah, saying:
I am the first and the last; I am he who liveth,
I am he who was slain;
I am your advocate with the Father.[19]

For members of The Church of Jesus Christ of Latter-day Saints—also part of the covenant family of Israel—*the Law* encompasses the fulness of the Gospel of Jesus Christ, which includes the Old and New Testaments, The Book of Mormon, The Doctrine and Covenants, and The Pearl of Great Price, as well as teachings of the modern prophets, and all covenants entered thereinto, including baptismal and temple covenants.

Do we love and honor the Law—the scriptures, commandments and covenants of the Lord?

Are we still in the process of receiving the Law in our lives?

---

1 Genesis 15:13–16.

2 Genesis 15:13–16; Exodus 2:24; Psalm 105:42; Acts 7:17.

3 Exodus 19:1–11.

4 Exodus 19:5.

5 1 Nephi 3:4

6 1 Nephi 5:11–14.

7 1 Nephi 5:21.

8 1 Nephi 4:2–3.

9 Rich, "Shavu'ot," *Judaism 101,* www.jewfaq.org.

10 Exodus 19:18.

11 Acts 2:3.

12 Acts 2:2.

13 Exodus 19:11.

14 Acts 2:6.

15 Acts 2:41.

16 Smith, *History of the Church* 2:432–33.

17 Anderson, "The Kirtland Temple—'A Pentecost and a Time of Rejoicing,'" *Meridian Magazine,* Sept. 24, 2021.

18 Doctrine and Covenants 110:11–13.

19 Doctrine and Covenants 110: 3–4.

CHAPTER 23

———— ∞◦∞ ————

Feast of Pentecost, *Shavuot:* The Betrothal of Jehovah to His People

I<small>N ADDITION TO CELEBRATING THE RECEPTION OF THE</small> L<small>AW AT</small> Pentecost, many teach that the events that took place at Mount Sinai, were, in fact, a betrothal of Israel, the Bride, to Jehovah, the Bridegroom. Israel Najara wrote the following in the 16ᵗʰ century:

> *The bridegroom delivered the Torah that is bigger*
> *than the earth and broader than the seas.*
> *The bride consented to the covenant,*
> *and an everlasting agreement was made.*
> *As a dowry, the bride brought a heart*
> *that understands, ears that listen, and eyes that see.[1]*

A betrothal implies that a wedding is yet to take place, and many who believe Jesus is the Bridegroom, look forward with joyful anticipation to that event.[2] However, we will see that a number of devout Jews also look forward to the long-promised wedding when Jehovah-God finally comes to meet and dwell with His people again. This hope is foreshadowed in the Feast of Tabernacles, which will be discussed later.

Diane Wolkstein explains:

Kabbalists believe that each section of the Bible that is studied on the evening of *Shavuot* adds a jewel or ornament to the bride, the people of Israel who will meet their bridegroom, God, the following day. During the service, before the Torah reading, Sephardic Jews read from a *ketubah* (a marriage contract) between God and the people, written in the sixteenth century by the mystic poet from Safed, Israel Najara:

> On the sixth day of the third month,
>   the Invisible One came forth from Sinai.
> The bridegroom, ruler of rulers, prince of princes,
>   said to his beloved (the people of Israel),
> who is beautiful as the moon, as radiant as the sun,
>   as awesome as an army with great banners,
> Many days you will be mine and I will be your redeemer.
> I will honor, support, and maintain you.
> I will be your shelter and refuge in eternal mercy.
> I will give you the Torah by which you and your children
>   will live in health and peace and harmony.
> May the Bridegroom rejoice with the Bride
> and the bride rejoice with the husband of her youth,
>   while uttering words of praise . . .
> At dawn, on the fiftieth day since they had left Egypt,
>   there was a long, loud blast of the ram's horn.
> The people came out of their tents
> and saw that every part of Mount Sinai was smoking.
> God had descended into the mountain.
> Thunder crashed over their heads.
> Lightning ripped through the air before their eyes.
> The ram's horn grew louder and louder.
> The people trembled. The mountain shook.
> Moses said, 'It is time to lead the bride to the bridegroom.'
> As Moses led the people to meet the Shechinah,
> Mount Sinai in exaltation lifted off the earth
> and hovered over the people like a wedding canopy.[3]

Brant Pitre explains:

From an ancient [Israelite] perspective, the one true God—"the LORD" or "He Who Is" (Hebrew YHWH)[4]—is not just the Creator. From an ancient (Israelite) perspective, the God of Israel is also a *Bridegroom*, a divine person whose ultimate desire is to be united to his creatures in an everlasting relationship that is so intimate, so permanent, so sacrificial, and so life-giving that it can only be described as a *marriage* between Creator and creatures, between God and human beings, between YHWH and Israel.[5]

Jehovah told His people: "I am married unto you."[6]

A review of ancient marriage customs might help us understand how the events at Mt. Sinai can be viewed as a betrothal of Jehovah to His people.

According to custom, a male emissary was chosen to act as the "friend of the bridegroom" and speak in his behalf to the bride and her parents, proposing marriage. The proposal would include negotiations for a dowry, as well as a bride-price—the "price" or gifts that the bridegroom would provide in order to secure the marriage. If the bride and her parents agreed, a *ketubah,* or contract, would be drawn up and signed, and the betrothal became official and binding.

The prospective bride was free to accept or reject the proposal.

With this perspective in mind, we can now recognize Moses in the role of the "friend of the Bridegroom," who presented the proposal to "the Bride," and when she accepted, he went back to report to his Friend.[7]

The scriptures begin to transform when we consider them in this light; they become love songs of the Lord as He proclaims: "Ye have seen . . . how I bare you on eagles' wings, and brought you unto myself. Now therefore, if ye will obey my voice indeed, and keep my covenant, then ye shall be a peculiar treasure unto me above all people: for all the earth is mine: And ye shall be unto me a kingdom of priests, and an holy nation."[8]

Out of all prospective brides, Jehovah chose Israel. Even the promise of being a "peculiar treasure unto me above all people" becomes beautiful. The Hebrew word *cegullah,* is a feminine word that signifies "property" in a special sense of a private possession one personally acquired and carefully preserves. Instead of today's interpretation of the word *peculiar* as "strange or odd," we might think of it in more specific terms, such as "you are my one and only, the one meant for me."

These terms should be interpreted as a free-will arrangement of intimacy, not ownership. This point is underscored in the proposed *if* of the overture: "*If* ye will . . ."[9]

The fact that Jehovah intended to exalt or lift His Bride, rather than to subject her to some form of slavery, is indicated by the promises contained within the proposal; He proposed that Israel become a kingdom of priests and a holy nation. In Hebrew the noun *kingdom* (*mamlakah*), is feminine, embracing both genders in the promise of exaltation. If they realize and accept what Jehovah is proposing, they will be raised to be kings and queens, priests and priestesses in His kingdom. Through His grace, they will become joint-heirs with Him[10] while yet recognizing that *He* is the King of kings and Lord of lords.[11]

Anciently, a prospective groom would offer gifts or *mattan* to his bride at the time of betrothal. These would often include bridal clothing, jewels, and precious coins that the bride would sew into a headband to wear on her wedding day. After the wedding, she would display the headband just inside the door of her home, so that all visitors to the home could witness the tokens of her husband's love for her.[12] The bridegroom might also present cash or services to the prospective bride's family.

Jehovah also gave gifts to *His* bride at Sinai: the glorious tabernacle/temple in which to prepare for His return, the beautiful priestly clothing in which to be adorned, and the precious Law, which, by following, His bride would surely be prepared for her eventual marriage to Him.

Although the Lord had intended that *all* of His people become kings and priests, and queens and priestesses, they were not yet ready to receive of the fulness of His covenant invitation.

Therefore, Levitical priests stood as proxy for the people in the tabernacle, foreshadowing each individual's future destiny, when—and if—they were ready to receive it. The priestly clothing was truly unique, particularly for a people who had just come out of slavery: white linen robes tied with white sashes and mites, or regal head coverings. Golden crowns engraved with the words "Holiness to the Lord" graced their foreheads. The high priest wore an ephod, or apron, embroidered in the royal colors of gold, blue, purple, and scarlet. Over his heart he wore a breastplate of gold and precious stones or jewels, and onyx and gold upon each shoulder.

Matthew Brown stated:

The fact that God Himself revealed the pattern for these vestments should alert us to the possibility that they imitate the clothing that is worn by heavenly beings.[13]

Isaiah said:

> I will greatly rejoice in the Lord,
> my soul shall be joyful in my God;
> for, he hath clothed me with the garments of salvation,
> he hath covered me with the robe of righteousness,
> as a bridegroom decketh himself with ornaments,
> and as a bride adorneth herself with her jewels.[14]

Today, in remembrance of the betrothal, and the anticipation of the future wedding, some women braid jewels into their hair on *Shavuot*, or Pentecost, and anoint themselves at dawn, symbolic of the bride preparing for the Bridegroom.

Are we prepared to meet the Bridegroom? Are we acknowledging and honoring the gifts He has given us, including temple ordinances, priestly clothing, and the Law and the covenant?

---

1 Najara, "Sephardic Marriage Contract." https://www.myjewishlearning.com/article/the-sha-vuot-marriage-contract/.

2 See Cherry, *The Redemption of the Bride: God's Redeeming Love for His Covenant People* for an in-depth exploration of this topic.

3 Wolkstein, *Treasures of the Heart: Holiday Stories that Reveal the Soul of Judaism*, 44, 51, 75–76.

4 Exodus 3:15.

5 Pitre, *Jesus the Bridegroom: The Greatest Love Story Ever Told*, 8.

6 Jeremiah 3:14.

7 Exodus 19:5–8; 33:11.

8 Exodus 19:4–8.

9 Exodus 19:5.

10 Romans 8:17.

11 Revelation 19:16.

12 Patai, *Sex and the Family in the Bible and the Middle East*, 57.

13 Brown, *The Gate of Heaven*, 81.

14 Isaiah 61:10.

—⟨⟩⟨⟩—

CHAPTER 24

The New and Everlasting Covenant—Invitation to a Covenant Fulness

And the Lord said unto Moses,
Lo, I come unto thee in a thick cloud,
that the people may hear when I speak with thee,
and believe thee forever.
And Moses told the words of the people unto the Lord.
And the Lord said unto Moses, Go unto the people,
and sanctify them today and tomorrow,
and let them wash their clothes,
And be ready against the third day:
for the third day the Lord will come down
in the sight of all the people upon mount Sinai.[1]

THERE IS PERHAPS NO MORE TRAGIC A STORY IN ALL OF SCRIP-ture than that which occurred at the foot of Mount Sinai, when the children of Israel refused the invitation to come up the mountain of the Lord and hear his voice, see Him, and know Him for themselves. They acted out of fear, and by doing so, they declined to enter into The New and Everlasting Covenant, which covenant contains a *fulness* of all blessings.[2]

The New and Everlasting Covenant is the fulness of the gospel of Jesus Christ.[3] "It is new every time it is revealed following a period of apostasy. It is everlasting in the sense that it is God's covenant and has been enjoyed in every gospel dispensation where people have been willing to receive it."[4] *Gospel Principles* explains:

> The fulness of the gospel is called the new and everlasting covenant. It includes the covenants made at baptism, during the sacrament, in the temple, and at any other time. The Lord calls it everlasting because it is ordained by an everlasting God and because the covenant will never be changed. He gave this same covenant to Adam, Enoch, Noah, Abraham, and other prophets. In this sense it is not new. But the Lord calls it new because each time the gospel is restored after being taken from the earth, it is new to the people who receive it.[5]

This New and Everlasting Covenant is the covenant Jehovah made with Abraham, and wanted to extend to Abraham's posterity at Mount Sinai, and to generations that followed. He wants to extend that same covenant to each one of us today.

A covenant is much more than a contract or a treaty; a covenant is a *relationship*. It represents the binding of one heart to another. The New and Everlasting Covenant—the eternal covenant God offers His people—represents the binding of God's heart to Israel and Israel's to God.

Israel is the name God gives to His covenant family. This is not linked directly to genetics or to bloodline but to those who accept and love God with all their heart, might, mind, and strength.

All "are alike unto God,"[6] and accepted into the covenant family regardless of their heritage.

This adoption of all who are willing to become a part of Israel is foreshadowed in the rituals associated with *Shavuot*, or Pentecost.

The Lord apparently intended to reveal Himself by degrees at Sinai. Protected from their sight by a thick cloud, the people could hear His voice as He spoke with Moses.[7] The declaration that "the Lord will come down in the sight of all the people upon Mount Sinai"[8] may be interpreted according to the various states of those present: they would hear or see only what they were prepared for. The footnote to Exodus 19:11 suggests a literal privilege of seeing God. This is the elevating promise of the covenant, and of the Melchizedek priesthood: that one may enter into His presence, and know Him for themselves:

And this greater priesthood administereth
the gospel and holdeth the key
to the mysteries of the kingdom,
even the key of the knowledge of God.
Therefore, in the ordinances thereof,
the power of godliness is manifest.
And without the ordinances thereof,
and the authority of the priesthood,
the power of godliness is not manifest unto men in the flesh;
For without this no man
can see the face of God, even the Father, and live.[9]

The Lord warned Moses that the people must not "break through" the barrier at the foot of the mountain, lest they "gaze" upon the Lord "and many of them perish" by coming into the light of His glory unprepared or unworthy.[10] Later, seventy elders, including Aaron and Joshua, *did* accept an invitation to enter the mount; they described seeing the "feet" and "hands" of God as they ate and drank with Him.[11] That was indeed a *fulness*!

Although they may have been *willing*, as evidenced by their declaration that "All that the Lord hath spoken we will do,"[12] the children of Israel were not then ready to receive the fulness of the gift that the Lord was offering to them. They were terrified by the lightning and thunder that accompanied the voice of the Lord, and His presence, and told Moses, "Speak thou with us, and we will hear: but let not God speak with us, lest we die."[13]

To make matters worse, while Moses was on the mount speaking face-to-face with the Lord,[14] the people, in their ignorance, fashioned a golden calf to worship.[15] 3,000 people died as a result of that abomination at Sinai,[16] and the children of Israel were forced to wander for forty years in the wilderness, until a faithful generation could be raised to finally enter the promised land.

The Lord referred to the Israelite's response to His invitation as "the Day of Provocation," and swore that they should not *"enter into His rest,"* or presence.[17] As a result, the Israelites lost the opportunity to obtain the priesthood of Abraham: the Melchizedek Priesthood. Without it, they *could not* enter into His rest.

Now this Moses plainly taught
to the children of Israel in the wilderness,
and sought diligently to sanctify his people
that they might behold the face of God;
But they hardened their hearts
and could not endure his presence;
therefore, the Lord in his wrath,
for his anger was kindled against them,
swore that they should not enter into his rest
while in the wilderness,
which rest is the fulness of his glory.
Therefore, he took Moses out of their midst,
and the Holy Priesthood also;
And the lesser priesthood continued,
which priesthood holdeth the key of the ministering of angels
and the preparatory gospel.[18]

We must not judge the Israelites at Sinai too harshly. They made an effort; they obeyed the instructions to wash and sanctify themselves, and took three days to ready their hearts and minds for their appointment with the Lord.[19] Moses had done everything within his power to prepare them, but they were unable to fully understand what they were being invited to do, and what they lost by their refusal.[20] They *did* accept a preparatory covenant,[21] although they were unable to comprehend and accept the fulness that Jehovah offered.

What is a fulness? And why should it be important to us?

Jehovah's encounter with Israel at Sinai is the first recorded event where a *group of people* were issued an invitation to enter into a covenant with the Lord and come to know Him intimately.

However, it is not the only occasion of its kind. The Savior issued several invitations to multitudes during His ministry in Palestine.[22] His visit to the Nephites had happier results; perhaps because the only people who survived the storms and earthquakes preceding His appearance were the "more righteous."[23] The Nephite response is the ultimate example of a people who were ready to receive, and the resulting miracles that can transpire when they do. Although many were present, the Savior had a one-on-one encounter with each individual.[24] We cannot help but feel that the same could have been had by each of the children of Israel at Sinai if they had not been so terrified. Salvation and atonement are not performed as a "group" event. A one-on-one encounter is what the Lord desires for all who "come unto Him."[25] This is the way we come to really *know* Him.

How have you had one-on-one encounters with the Lord? Have you seen a progression in knowledge—knowing—Him as a result?

Although the preceding groups were invited to be eyewitnesses, King Benjamin's people did not require such an experience before manifesting their faith. They prepared themselves and heeded the teachings of their prophet-king. When he invited them to enter into a covenant with Jesus Christ, they were eager to accept the privilege of doing so.[26] "Blessed are they that have not seen, and yet have believed."[27]

> *For whoso is faithful*
> *unto the obtaining these two priesthoods*
> *of which I have spoken, and the magnifying their calling,*
> *are sanctified by the Spirit*
> *unto the renewing of their bodies.*
> *They become the sons of Moses and of Aaron*
> *and the seed of Abraham*
> *and the church and kingdom, and the elect of God.*
> *And also all they who receive this priesthood* **receive me,**
> *saith the Lord;*
> *For he that receiveth my servants receiveth me;*
> *And he that receiveth me receiveth my Father;*
> *And he that receiveth my Father*
> *receiveth my Father's kingdom;*
> *therefore all that my Father hath shall be given unto him.*
> *And this is according to the oath and covenant*
> *which belongeth to the priesthood.*[28]

In His continued mercy, the Lord has time and again sought to restore the same promised blessings that come with the fulness of The New and Everlasting Covenant. Our day is yet another day of invitation. Joseph Smith, the prophet of the Dispensation of the Fulness of Times, has been the prophet-messenger of the Restoration. Again, the

Lord issues an invitation from His "holy mount"—the temple—to enter into covenant with Him and receive a fulness.

As with the Israelites, some members of the Church may be content to stay at the foot of the "mount," outside the temple gates, and send the current prophet (and others) to speak to the Lord in their behalf.

Paul urges: "Let us therefore fear, lest, a promise being left us of entering into his rest, [remember what "rest" is!] any of you should seem to come short of it. For unto us was the gospel preached, as well as unto them: but the word preached did not profit them, not being mixed with faith in them that heard it. . . . Let us labour therefore to enter into that rest, lest any man fall after the same example of unbelief."[29]

President Russell M. Nelson said:

The Church of Jesus Christ of Latter-day Saints has been restored in these latter days to fulfill ancient promises of the Lord. It is part of the "restitution of all things." Committed children of the covenant remain steadfast, even in the midst of adversity. We shall "be chastened and tried, even as Abraham, who was commanded to offer up his only son." Yet we are strengthened by this promise of the Lord: "Ye are lawful heirs, according to the flesh, and have been hid from the world with Christ in God—Therefore your life and the priesthood have remained, and must needs remain through you and your lineage until the restoration of all things. . . . Therefore, blessed are ye if ye continue in my goodness, a light unto the Gentiles, and through this priesthood, a savior unto my people Israel."[30]

The Lord has said: "I covenanted with Abraham that I would remember his seed forever."[31] *We, as children of Abraham, must come to know what that promise means.*

And I will make of thee a great nation,
and I will bless thee above measure,
and make thy name great among all nations,
and thou shalt be a blessing unto thy seed after thee,
that in their hands they shall bear this ministry
and Priesthood unto all nations;

And I will bless them through thy name;
for as many as receive this Gospel shall be called after thy name,
and shall be accounted thy seed,
and shall rise up and bless thee, as their father;
. . .and in thy seed (that is, thy Priesthood),
for I give unto thee a promise
that this right shall continue in thee,
and in thy seed after thee . . .
shall all the families of the earth be blessed,
even with the blessings of the Gospel,
which are the blessings of salvation, even of life eternal.[32]

May we ever seek to obtain the promised blessings, and accept the Lord's invitation to come into the fulness of the covenant, not holding back in fear, but with perfect hope, press forward in faith and trust in Him who is "mighty to save."[33]

---

1 Exodus 19:9–11.

2 Doctrine and Covenants 22:1; 131:2; 132:6.

3 Doctrine and Covenants 66:2.

4 "New and everlasting covenant," *The Guide to the Scriptures*.

5 "The Lord's Covenant People," *Gospel Principles*.

6 2 Nephi 26:33.

7 Exodus 19:9.

8 Exodus 19:11.

9 Doctrine and Covenants 84:19–22.

10 Exodus 19:21, 23; see Deuteronomy 4:12, The "smoke" that accompanied the Lord is cross-referenced to mean "glory," see Exodus 24:17; Deuteronomy 5:22–27; Isaiah 6:4.

11 Exodus 24:1, 10–11.

12 Exodus 19:8.

13 Exodus 20:18–19.

14 Exodus 33:11.

15 Exodus 32:1–7.

16 Exodus 32:28.

17 Psalm 95:8–11; Hebrews 3:8; Jacob 1:7.

18 Doctrine and Covenants 84:23–26.

19 Exodus 19:10.

20 Doctrine and Covenants 84:14–24.

21 Doctrine and Covenants 84:26.

22 See Matthew 5–7; 11:28.

23 3 Nephi 9:13; 10:22.

24 3 Nephi 11:15.

25 John 14:23; 1 Nephi 10:18; 15:14; 2 Nephi 26:33.

26 See Mosiah 1–6.

27 John 20:29.

28 Doctrine and Covenants 84:33–39.

29 Hebrews 4:1–2, 11.

30 Doctrine and Covenants 86:9-11; Nelson, "Children of the Covenant," Apr. 1995 General Conference.

31 2 Nephi 29:14.

32 Abraham 2:9–11

33 Isaiah 63:1.

CHAPTER 25

―――――⟐―――――

Feast of Pentecost, *Shavuot*, Work Chart

WHAT ARE YOUR THOUGHTS ABOUT PENTECOST, *SHAVUOT?* How can you use the following chart to prepare yourself to constantly receive the law and honor your covenants?

PENTECOST (*SHAVUOT*)—50 DAYS AFTER PASSOVER

Item	Application	Additional Insight
Remembrance of receiving the Law at Sinai		
Betrothal of Jehovah to His People		
Devout Jews stay awake all night reading the Torah	Symbolic of desire to "receive" and honor the Law	

Item	Application	Additional Insight
Women anoint themselves; braid jewels in hair	Church to be ready and prepared as a bride for Second Coming	
Two loaves of leavened bread	Two "sinful" people presented: House of Israel and Gentiles	
Book of Ruth read	Ruth, a Gentile, progenitor of the Savior; adopted Israel	
Two lambs presented with the two loaves for a peace offering		
Seven lambs, one bullock, two rams, and a scapegoat part of the sacrifices and rituals		
Ram's horn "sounded"	Believed to be the horn from the ram provided at Isaac's sacrifice, represents the voice of the Lord.	
Invitation to Covenant		

Shavuot AND Pentecost—
Ex. 19, 32; Acts 2; D&C 110

At Mt. Sinai	Day of Pentecost	Kirtland Temple
Mountain filled with smoke; Lord descended upon it in fire	The room was filled with cloven tongues of fire	Glory filled the temple; heavenly visitors
A trumpet sounded to call the people	A sound from heaven filled the upper room	Sound of rushing wind
All was done "in the sight of the people"	"all the people of the city" were drawn to the apostles and the wind, sounds, etc.	People from nearby saw angels on the rooftop
3,000 people killed for idolatry	3,000 people saved and baptized	Keys restored to bring salvation to all mankind

CHAPTER 26

The Feast of Trumpets,
Rosh Hashanah

And in the seventh month, on the first day of the month,
you shall have a holy convocation:
you shall do no manner of servile work;
it is a day of blowing the trumpets unto you.[1]

BLOW THE TRUMPETS! WAKE UP WORLD! IT'S TIME TO AWAKE AND prepare for the coming of the Bridegroom-Messiah!

The Feast of Trumpets, or *Rosh Hashanah*, is the first of the three fall feasts that celebrate the final harvests of the year, and foreshadow the harvest of souls preparatory to the arrival of the Messiah, who will dwell with His people for a thousand years.

The Feast of Trumpets also signals a ten-day period of repentance that culminates with *Yom Kippur*, or The Day of Atonement. This ten-day period is appropriately referred to as the *Days of Awe*.

The blowing of trumpets was a serious and sacred duty in ancient times. Watchmen were appointed to stand on towers throughout the land, and sound their trumpets in warning when danger approached. If the watchman sounded the alarm at the appropriate time, he was relieved of any responsibility for individuals who did not heed the warning. However, if he did not sound the alarm, the blood that ensued would be "on his head," or, in other words, God would hold him responsible for the death and disaster that occurred to his people. Likewise, if the trumpet were sounded, and a person did not heed the warning, the watchman was free of responsibility, and the liability would be upon the person who did not listen and respond accordingly.[2]

The sounding of the trumpet was associated with the voice of the Lord since the day of Pentecost at Mt. Sinai.[3] Different forms of trumpets, including those made of silver and gold, were used in temple services from the time of the construction of the tabernacle. The *shofar*, or ram's horn, was considered to be particularly sacred, and associated with God's voice calling to His people. The *shofar* is associated with the ram found in the thicket at the time of Abraham's proposed sacrifice of his son, Isaac. God provided the ram in the place of Isaac, and so the call of the ram's horn reminds those that hear it of the Lord's atoning mercy and love.

God calls to His people in warning, but with a voice of love and compassion. The Feast of Trumpets particularly illustrates this truth as it prepares Israel to wake up and prepare for the coming Messiah by repenting and cleansing one's life, and gathering as families into the shelter of the *sukkah* (Feast of Tabernacles), and into the presence of God.

All three trumpets—silver, gold, and the *shofar*—were blown on the Feast of Trumpets. According to the Temple Institute in Jerusalem, the *shofar* was to sound longer than the other trumpets, "as the chief commandment of the day is to hear the *shofar*."[4]

In beautiful imagery, the Temple Institute teaches that the blowing of the *shofar* on *Rosh Hashanah* symbolizes the commemoration of God blowing His breath into Adam—and that both events, the creation of Adam and the sacrifice of Isaac—took place on Mt. Moriah, the very spot where the ancient temple stood in Jerusalem. They also believe that Adam's first sacrifice of repentance took place at that same sacred location.[5]

As stated previously, The Feast of Trumpets, *Rosh Hashanah*, was to signal a time of preparation for the holiest day of the year, *Yom Kippur*, or The Day of Atonement. The question on each person's mind was whether or not their name would be written in the Book of Life. As we are all children of Adam and Eve, the Temple Institute explains:

Rosh Hashanah is the day that we recognize the sovereignty of God the King, Creator of the universe and Judge of all mankind. The day on which "all beings pass before Him like tender sheep," *Rosh Hashanah's* message is truly universal: it is incumbent upon all mankind to accept upon ourselves God's sovereignty, and to take account of our thoughts and actions, in light of this awesome recognition.[6]

It is taught that one's name is inscribed in the Book of Life or of Death on the Feast of Trumpets, but that it is "sealed" in one of those books on The Day of Atonement. There is a ten-day period in which to adjust the initial judgment through repentance, prayer, and good deeds. "A common greeting during this time is 'May you be inscribed and sealed for a good year.'"[7]

Tradition held that "on *Rosh Hashanah*, when the Lord hears the call of the *Shofar*, He rises from His throne of justice and sits on His throne of mercy."[8]

Rabbi Chaim Richman, urges:

God looks for the good in all of us. He seeks to bestow His benevolence on man. But ultimately, life is about the choices we continue to make at every moment. It's all up to us . . . We live in a bold new world, one that requires us to make bold choices. The first choice is to choose life. It is not the Holy One, blessed be He, who will write us into the book of life, or, Heaven forbid, the opposite— it is we ourselves who make the choice, through our actions, and write our own names into the book of our choice.[9]

Rosh Hashanah was a second new year for the Israelites (Passover also being considered a new year), and as such, it marked a new beginning, even as one can become a "new man" or a "new woman" through repenting and "beginning again."

Rosh Hashanah also marked the beginning of the final harvest, which would be celebrated fifteen days later, with *Sukkot*, or *The Feast of Tabernacles*.

The opportunity to reflect upon our standing before God helps us to focus our hearts and minds upon Him; these holy days offer a beautiful opportunity to stop and consider, and make needed adjustments in our preparations to meet the Lord.

Can we hear the sound of the trumpet, saying "Awake! Awake!"?

1 Numbers 29:1.

2 Ezekiel 33:2–5.

3 Exodus 19:19.

4 "The Holy Temple: Rosh Hashana," *Temple Institute,* templeinstitute.org/rosh-hashana.

5 Ibid.

6 Ibid.

7 Rich, "Days of Awe," *Judaism 102,* https://www.jewfaq.org.

8 Vayikra Raba, 29:10.

9 Chaim Richman, email message to author, September 12, 2007.

CHAPTER 27

—⁓⁓—

The Feast of Trumpets and
The Book of Mormon

And I saw another angel fly in the midst of heaven,
having the everlasting gospel to preach
unto them that dwell on the earth,
and to every nation, and kindred, and tongue, and people,
Saying with a loud voice,
Fear God, and give glory to him;
for the hour of his judgment is come:
and worship him that made heaven, and earth,
and the sea, and the fountains of waters.[1]

FOUR YEARS AFTER FIRST SHOWING JOSEPH SMITH WHERE THE golden plates were buried, the angel Moroni told Joseph he could finally take possession of them and begin the work of translation of The Book of Mormon.[2] That date was September 22, 1827—The Feast of Trumpets.

If the Lord used the Feast of Trumpets, *Rosh Hashanah*, to signal His people to awake to His voice, repent, and prepare for the coming of the Messiah and the final harvest of souls, The Book of Mormon is the perfect instrument of fulfillment. As a "voice from the dust,"[3] Isaiah prophesied that even the "deaf [will] hear the words of the book."[4] And, let us not forget, that Moroni is always portrayed with a trumpet in his hand, sounding the warning and the call to all Israel to come to the Lord in His holy mount—the temple.

The Church of Jesus Christ of Latter-day Saints is a *restoration*. As has been previously discussed, The New and Everlasting Covenant is the same covenant given to Adam and Eve, to Abraham and Sarah, and to the heads of each dispensation who would receive it. It includes priesthood keys and authority, and the ordinances of salvation that are administered therein.

Those keys and ordinances, together with sacred doctrines inherent in the covenant have been restored today through the prophet Joseph Smith.

The theme of covenant promises runs like a golden thread in the rich tapestry of the scriptures, including the Bible and The Book of Mormon. When Moroni first appeared to Joseph Smith, he quoted the promise of Malachi 4:5–6, but with important changes: "Behold, I will reveal unto you the Priesthood, by the hand of Elijah the prophet, before the coming of the great and dreadful day of the Lord. And he shall plant in the hearts of the children *the promises* made to the fathers, and the hearts of the children shall turn to their fathers. If it were not so, the whole earth would be utterly wasted at his coming."[5]

These covenant promises have been in effect since they were first made with Adam and Eve, renewed with Abraham, Isaac, and Jacob, and carried down through the ages. The Lord's faithfulness to His end of the covenant promises is one of the greatest witnesses of His mercy.

The realization of the covenant promises is possible only through the Father's Plan of Salvation, and the Atonement of the Savior, Jesus Christ. Despite the fact that generations fell away from the covenants their progenitors made, *because of the faithfulness* of parents like Adam and Eve, Abraham and Sarah, and Lehi and Sariah, covenant promises continued to be extended to their posterity . . . and to us today.

The Title Page of The Book of Mormon explains the book's role in restoring and remembering the covenants made to the House of Israel:

> Wherefore, it is an abridgment of the record of the people of Nephi, and also of the Lamanites—Written to the Lamanites, who are a remnant of the house of Israel; and also to the Jew and Gentile—
>
> . . . Which is to show unto the remnant of the house of Israel what great things the Lord hath done for their fathers; and that they may know the covenants of the Lord, that they are not cast off forever—And also to the convincing of the Jew and Gentile that

JESUS is the CHRIST, the ETERNAL GOD, manifesting himself unto all nations—And now, if there are faults they are the mistakes of men; wherefore, condemn not the things of God, that ye may be found spotless at the judgment-seat of Christ.

The Book of Mormon not only witnesses to covenant promises made in the past, but it is also a tool by which Abraham's posterity is gathered in to the covenant today. President Russell M. Nelson taught:

Anciently, the Lord blessed Father Abraham with a promise to make his posterity a chosen people. References to this covenant occur throughout the scriptures. Included were promises that the Son of God would come through Abraham's lineage, that certain lands would be inherited, that nations and kindreds of the earth would be blessed through his seed, and more. While some aspects of that covenant have already been fulfilled, the Book of Mormon teaches that this Abrahamic covenant will be fulfilled only in these latter days! It also emphasizes that we are among the covenant people of the Lord. Ours is the privilege to participate personally in the fulfillment of these promises. What an exciting time to live!

Russell M. Nelson continued:

The coming forth of the Book of Mormon is a sign to the entire world that the Lord has commenced to gather Israel and fulfill covenants He made to Abraham, Isaac, and Jacob. We not only teach this doctrine, but we participate in it.

. . . The Book of Mormon is central to this work. It declares the doctrine of the gathering. It causes people to learn about Jesus Christ, to believe His gospel, and to join His Church. In fact, if there were no Book of Mormon, the promised gathering of Israel would not occur.

. . . To us the honored name of *Abraham* is important. It is mentioned in more verses of scriptures of the Restoration than in all verses of the Bible. Abraham is linked to all members of The Church of Jesus Christ of Latter-day Saints. The Lord reaffirmed the Abrahamic covenant in our day through the Prophet Joseph Smith. In the temple we receive our ultimate blessings, as the seed of Abraham, Isaac, and Jacob.[6]

As the trumpets blown on The Feast of Trumpets signal, the Lord is calling His people to awake, to remember, to repent, and to prepare themselves for the coming Messiah. The Book of Mormon shares this identical message, and reassures all of Israel, even as its members are scattered and forgetful of their heritage, that the Lord has not forgotten them. Mormon testifies that when the Book of Mormon begins to go forth, ". . . ye may know that the covenant which the Father hath made with the children of Israel, concerning their restoration to the lands of their inheritance, is already beginning to be fulfilled. And ye may know that the words of the Lord, which have been spoken by the holy prophets, shall all be fulfilled; and ye need not say that the Lord delays his coming unto the children of Israel. And ye need not imagine in your hearts that the words which have been spoken are vain, for behold, the Lord will remember his covenant which he hath made unto his people of the house of Israel."[7]

---

1 Revelation 14:6–7.
2 Joseph Smith History 1:59.
3 2 Nephi 26:15–16.
4 Isaiah 29:18.
5 Doctrine and Covenants 2.
6 Nelson, "The Gathering of Scattered Israel," Oct. 2006 General Conference, emphasis added.
7 3 Nephi 29:1–3.

CHAPTER 28

──── ⟡ ────

Feast of Trumpets Work Chart

Now that you have had some practice with the charts, you will find that the interpretations and applications are left blank for you. You may find new meaning each time you ponder and consider what the Spirit is teaching you for your life at this moment.

Feast of Trumpets

Symbol	Christ	Personal Insight/ Application
Silver and gold trumpets sound		
Shofar most important and sounds long and daily		
Ten-day period of Repentance "Days of Awe"		

Symbol	Christ	Personal Insight/ Application
Name written in Book of Life or Death—to be "sealed" on Day of Atonement		
Beginning of the Final Harvest		
Prepare for the Coming of the Lord		
Joseph Smith received the plates of the Book of Mormon on Feast of Trumpets		
Remember covenants of Adam, Eve, Abraham, and Sarah		
A New Year		

CHAPTER 29

The Day of Atonement, *Yom Kippur*

Also on the tenth day of this seventh month there shall be a day of atonement:
it shall be an holy convocation unto you;
and ye shall afflict your souls,
and offer an offering made by fire unto the Lord.
And ye shall do no work in that same day:
for it is a day of atonement,
to make an atonement for you before the Lord your God.¹

YOM KIPPUR, OR THE DAY OF ATONEMENT IS CONSIDERED TO BE the most holy day of all of the sacred feasts. It takes place on the tenth day of Tishri, following a period of repentance that begins with the blowing of the *shofar* on *Rosh Hashanah*, the Feast of Trumpets.

During the ten-day period of reflection, each individual seeks to cleanse the inner vessel, to set aside the sins and pollution of the world, and to qualify himself/herself for a reunion with God, as symbolized by the special rituals performed on the Day of Atonement. Only on this one day of the year was the high priest permitted to enter within the Holy of Holies in behalf of all of Israel. And, on this day, it was believed, one's judgment was "sealed" in the Book of Life or Death.

The blowing of the *shofar* was repeated throughout the ten days, as well as on The Day of Atonement. Anciently, the *shofar* was to be blown with thirty blasts, which later evolved to one hundred. A specific pattern was to be followed for these *Days of Awe* that varied the length of the blasts. People described some of the sounds as moaning, or grief-filled. One writer suggests that the various sounds proclaimed: "We are desperate for God. . . . We are brokenhearted over

167

our separation from God." He went on to say: "And the final blast . . . is God's response of love, saying, 'Return, My children, return. No matter where you roam, you can always come back home.'"[2]

All of Israel would gather at the temple in response to the *shofar's* call on The Day of Atonement. The events that transpired were symbolically rich and deeply somber. It was thought that if the high priest entered the Holy of Holies unworthily, he would die, based on the Lord's warning that Aaron should not come in at any other time in the year "that he die not."[3] As the high priest made restitution not only for himself, but for each priest and worshipper, these took their individual responsibilities seriously, and sought earnestly for repentance and redemption. This was a day of fasting, prayer, and great preparation. One did not come to the temple hurried, harried, or distracted.

The Day was unique in many ways, including the specific duties of the high priest, the manner of the sacrifices made, and the ritual of the scapegoat.

> *Speak unto Aaron thy brother, that he come not at all times into the holy place within the veil before the mercy seat, which is upon the ark; that he die not; for I will appear in the cloud upon the mercy seat. Thus shall Aaron come into the holy place: with a young bullock for a sin offering, and a ram for a burnt offering. He shall put on the holy linen coat, and he shall have the linen breeches upon his flesh, and shall be girded with a linen girdle, and with the linen mitre shall he be attired: these are holy garments; therefore shall he wash his flesh in water, and so put them on.*[4]

The high priest was distinguished on every other day by the "golden garments" and vestments he wore. This included the colorful ephod with its accompanying breastplate bearing precious stones, one for each tribe of Israel, the epaulets on each shoulder, also with precious stones, and the golden headband inscribed "Holiness to the Lord." On the Day of Atonement, the high priest was to wash and change his clothing numerous times throughout the day, officiating primarily in the clothing of the "ordinary" priest—white linen garments—and without the finery that set him apart on all other occasions. He was to make expiation not only for the implements of the temple, the priests that served therein, the congregants without, but also for himself and his family. In this capacity, he set aside his beautiful golden garments that distinguished him on all other days, and wore simple white garments, that would be disposed of at the end of the day's services. And, he was also required to perform all of the sacrifices of the day—including the ordinary daily sacrifices—alone. Preparations had been made for this sacred occasion for more than a week in advance. He was to stay awake all night long before the great Day, hearing and expounding scriptures, and preparing himself so that he might enter within the Holy of Holies worthily.

Alfred Edersheim explains:

> The services of the day began with the first streak of morning light. Already the people had been admitted into the sanctuary. So jealous were they of any innovation or alteration, that only a linen cloth excluded the high priest from public view, when each time before changing his garments, he bathed—not in the ordinary place of priests, but in one specially set apart for his use. Altogether he changed his raiments and washed his whole body five times on that day, and his hands and feet ten times. When the first dawn of morning was announced in the usual manner, the high priest put off his ordinary (layman's) dress, bathed, put on his golden vestments, washed his hands and feet, and proceeded to perform all of the principal parts of the ordinary morning service. The morning service finished, the high priest washed his hands and feet, put off his golden vestments, bathed, put on his "linen garments," again washed his hands and feet, and proceeded to the peculiar part of the day's services.[5]

The "peculiar" services that Edersheim references were most unique, indeed, and required the high priest to travel from one place to another within the courtyard, the Holy Place and the Holy of Holies, as if he were setting a stage before performing the actual sacrifice or ritual. Each movement was deliberate, and had been given in specific detail by the Lord Himself:

> *And he shall take of the congregation of the children of Israel two kids of the goats for a sin offering, and one ram for a burnt offering. And Aaron shall offer his bullock of the sin offering which is for himself,*

and make atonement for himself and for his house. And he shall take the two goats, and present them before the Lord at the door of the tabernacle of the congregation. And Aaron shall cast lots upon the two goats; one lot for the Lord, and the other lot for the scapegoat. And Aaron shall bring the goat upon which the Lord's lot fell, and offer him for a sin offering. But the goat, on which the lot fell to be the scapegoat, shall be presented alive before the Lord, to make an atonement with him, and to let him go for a scapegoat into the wilderness.

And Aaron shall bring the bullock of the sin offering, which is for himself, and shall make an atonement for himself, and for his house, and shall kill the bullock of the sin offering which is for himself: And he shall take a censer full of burning coals of fire from off the altar before the Lord, and his hands full of sweet incense beaten small, and bring it within the veil: And he shall put the incense upon the fire before the Lord, that the cloud of the incense may cover the mercy seat that is upon the testimony, that he die not:

And he shall take of the blood of the bullock, and sprinkle it with his finger upon the mercy seat eastward; and before the mercy seat shall he sprinkle of the blood with his finger seven times.

Then shall he kill the goat of the sin offering, that is for the people, and bring his blood within the veil, and do with the blood as he did with the blood of the bullock, and sprinkle it upon the mercy seat, and before the mercy seat: And he shall make an atonement for the holy place, because of the uncleanness of the children of Israel, and because of their transgressions in all their sins: and so shall he do for the tabernacle of the congregation, that remaineth among them in the midst of their uncleanness.

And there shall be no man in the tabernacle of the congregation when he goeth in to make an atonement in the holy place, until he come out, and have made an atonement for himself, and for his household, and for all the congregation of Israel.

And he shall go out unto the altar that is before the Lord, and make an atonement for it; and shall take of the blood of the bullock, and of the blood of the goat, and put it upon the horns of the altar round about. And he shall sprinkle of the blood upon it with his finger seven times, and cleanse it, and hallow it from the uncleanness of the children of Israel.

And when he hath made an end of reconciling the holy place, and the tabernacle of the congregation, and the altar, he shall bring the live goat: And Aaron shall lay both his hands upon the head of the live goat, and confess over him all the iniquities of the children of Israel, and all their transgressions in all their sins, putting them upon the head of the goat, and shall send him away by the hand of a fit man into the wilderness: And the goat shall bear upon him all their iniquities unto a land not inhabited: and he shall let go the goat in the wilderness.

And Aaron shall come into the tabernacle of the congregation, and shall put off the linen garments, which he put on when he went into the holy place, and shall leave them there: And he shall wash his flesh with water in the holy place, and put on his garments, and come forth, and offer his burnt offering, and the burnt offering of the people, and make an atonement for himself, and for the people.

And the fat of the sin offering shall he burn upon the altar. And he that let go the goat for the scapegoat shall wash his clothes, and bathe his flesh in water, and afterward come into the camp.

And the bullock for the sin offering, and the goat for the sin offering, whose blood was brought in to make atonement in the holy place, shall one carry forth without the camp; and they shall burn in the fire their skins, and their flesh, and their dung. And he that burneth them shall wash his clothes, and bathe his flesh in water, and afterward he shall come into the camp.

And this shall be a statute forever unto you: that in the seventh month, on the tenth day of the month, ye shall afflict your souls, and do no work at all, whether it be one of your own country, or a stranger that sojourneth among you: For on that day shall the priest make an atonement for you, to cleanse you, that ye may be clean from all your sins before the Lord. It shall be a Sabbath of rest unto you, and ye shall afflict your souls, by a statute forever.

And the priest, whom he shall anoint, and whom he shall consecrate to minister in the priest's office in his father's stead, shall make the atonement, and shall put on the linen clothes, even the holy garments: And he shall make an atonement for the holy sanctuary, and he shall make an atonement for the tabernacle of the congregation, and for the altar, and he shall make an atonement for the priests, and for all the people of the congregation. And this shall be an everlasting statute unto you, to make an atonement for the children of Israel for all their sins once a year.[6]

The first ritual of confession and expiation was to be performed in behalf of the high priest and his family. The priest could not act in behalf of his congregation without first ensuring that he was right with the Lord. This is an important principle to remember when acting in any leadership role. "Be ye clean, that bear the vessels of the Lord."[7]

Edersheim offers some helpful perspective:

> The high priest purchased from his own funds the sacrifices brought for himself and his house. The bullock for his (own) sin-offering stood between the Temple-porch and the altar. It was placed towards the south, but the high priest, who stood facing the east (that is, the worshippers), turned the head of the sacrifice towards the west (that is, to face the sanctuary). He then laid both his hands upon the head of the bullock, and confessed as follows:—"Ah, JEHOVAH! I have committed iniquity; I have transgressed; I have sinned—I and my house. Oh, then JEHOVAH, I entreat Thee, cover over (atone for, let there be atonement for) the iniquities, the transgressions, and the sins which I have committed, transgressed, and sinned before Thee, I and my house—even as it is written in the law of Moses, Thy servant: 'For, on that day will He cover over (atone) for you to make a you clean; from all your transgressions before JEHOVAH ye shall be cleansed.'"
>
> It will be noticed that in this solemn confession the name JEHOVAH occurred three times. Other three times was it pronounced in the confession which the high-priest made over the same bullock for the priesthood; a seventh time was it uttered when he cast the lot as to which of the two goats as to be "for JEHOVAH;" and once again he spoke it three times in the confession over the so-called "scape-goat" which bore the sins of the people. All these ten times the high priest pronounced the very name JEHOVAH, and as he spoke it, those who stood near cast themselves with their faces on the ground, while the multitude responded: "Blessed be the Name; the glory of His kingdom is for ever and ever."[8]

Once the confession and expiation had been made for the priest, the services turned towards an atonement in behalf of the people. Two goats were brought into the courtyard, their backs facing the people, and their heads facing the temple. Lots where drawn, one bearing the inscription "for Jehovah," and the other "for *Azazel*" (Hebrew for "scapegoat"). With both hands, the high priest drew the lots from an urn—one in his left hand and one in his right hand—as he faced the congregation, one goat on the left and one on the right. The lots were placed accordingly on each of the goats, their fate having been decided. The high priest then tied a scarlet piece of cloth around the horn of the scapegoat, and another around the throat of the goat destined for temple sacrifice.

The scapegoat was then turned around to face the people whose sins he would figuratively be carrying into the wilderness, and the high priest was on to his next order of service. He laid his hands upon the bullock that had earlier been made proxy for his own sins and those of his family, and repeated once again the initial blessing of transference, but now also included a prayer of transference in behalf of all the priests who ministered in the temple. The high priest then killed the bullock, catching its blood in a vessel for use later in the procedures.

The high priest moved in a veritable ceremonial dance, as he now turned to the altar of burnt-offering, filled a censer with burning coals, and took a handful of frankincense that he would add to the coals once inside the Holy of Holies. He carried these into the Holy Place, and out of sight of the congregation. He then placed the censer of coals on the foundation stone within the Holy of Holies, and threw the frankincense into the flames. The Lord's awe-inspiring instructions for this part of the ritual were, "And he shall put the incense upon the fire before the Lord, that the cloud of the incense may cover the mercy seat that is upon the testimony, that he die not."[9]

The "mercy seat that is upon the testimony" refers to the Ark of the Covenant, which held the tablets of stone containing the commandments written by the finger of the Lord at Sinai. It also contained Aaron's rod of priesthood authority, and a container of manna. The top of the Ark was called the throne of God, or "the mercy seat," and held a central role in the services of The Day of Atonement.

Once the smoke of the incense had filled the Holy of Holies, Aaron returned to the courtyard, to take up the vessel containing the bullock's blood. He once again turned to enter within the veil and into the Holy of Holies, where he dipped his finger and sprinkled blood on the mercy seat, seven times upward and seven times downward. After completing that ritual, he placed the bowl with the blood just before the veil, and made his way back again, into the courtyard, where he completed the sacrifice of the goat "meant for Jehovah." He took the vessel containing its blood and repeated the procedure he had performed earlier with the blood of the bullock: seven times upward and seven times downward, sprinkling the blood upon the mercy seat. When he finished, he placed the bowl with the goat's blood on a golden stand before the veil.

His duties were not yet completed. Back he went with the bullock's blood to repeat what he had done previously: seven times up and seven times down, sprinkling the blood on the mercy seat, the throne of God. He followed the same pattern with the goat's blood once again, and then, at last, combined the blood of both animals, and used it to sprinkle the horns of the altar of incense, which stood just before the veil in the Holy Place. He then sprinkled seven times up and seven times down over the entire altar of incense. In performing these rituals, the high priest purified the sanctuary in all of its parts from the sins of the people and the priests.

Edersheim explains:

> By these expiatory sprinklings the high priest had cleansed the sanctuary in all its parts from the defilement of the priesthood and the worshippers. The Most Holy Place, the veil, the Holy Place, the altar of incense, and the altar of burnt-offering were now clean alike, so far as the priesthood and as the people were concerned; and in their relationship to the sanctuary both priests and worshippers were atoned for. So far as the law could give it, there was now again free access for all; or, to put it otherwise, the continuance of typical sacrificial communion with God was once more restored and secured. Had it not been for these services, it would have become impossible for priests and people to offer sacrifices, and so to obtain the forgiveness of sins, or to have fellowship with God. But the consciences were not yet free from a sense of personal guilt and sin. That remained to be done through the "scape goat."

Most solemn as the services had hitherto been, the worshippers would chiefly think with awe of the high priest going into the immediate presence of God, coming out alive, and securing for them by the blood the continuance of the Old Testament privileges of sacrifices and of access unto God through them. What now took place concerned them, if possible, even more nearly.

Their own personal guilt and sins were now to be removed from them, and that in a symbolical rite, at one and the same time the most mysterious and most significant of all. All the while the "scape goat" with the "scarlet tongue" telling of its guilt it was to bear, had stood looking eastwards, confronting the people, and waiting for the terrible load which it was to carry away "unto a land not inhabited." Laying both his hands on the head of this goat, the high priest now confessed and pleaded: "Ah, JEHOVAH! They have committed iniquity; they have transgressed; they have sinned—Thy people, the house of Israel. Oh, then, JEHOVAH! Cover over (atone for), I intreat Thee, upon their iniquities, their transgressions, and their sins, which they have wickedly committed, transgressed, and sinned before Thee—Thy people, the house of Israel. As it is written in the law of Moses, Thy servant, saying: 'For on that day shall it be covered over (atoned) for you, to make you clean from all your sins before JEHOVAH ye shall be cleansed.'"

And while the prostrate multitude worshipped at the name of Jehovah, the high priest turned his face towards them as he uttered the last words, "Ye shall be cleansed!" as if to declare them the absolution and remission of their sins.[10]

The remaining "scapegoat" was then led through the eastern gate, which opened towards the Mount of Olives, and taken into the wilderness. It appears that in the earliest years, the scapegoat wandered unscathed in the wilderness, but at some point, priests sought to ensure the death of the goat by pushing it from a cliff. They didn't want it wandering back into town bearing its scarlet cloth of accusation against them. Before sending the goat to its death, the ribbon of red cloth was torn into two pieces: one part to remain tied to the goat, and the other to tie to the cliff or to the door of the temple. Once the remaining cloth had turned white, the people understood that their sins had been forgiven, in relation to Isaiah's prophecy: "Come now, and let us reason together, saith the Lord; though your sins be as scarlet, they shall be white as snow; though they be red like crimson, they shall be as wool."[11]

---

1 Leviticus 23:27–28.

2 "The Mysteries of the Shofar," *House of David Ministries.*

3 Leviticus 16:2.

4 Leviticus 16:2–4.

5 Edersheim, *The Temple: Its Ministry and Service,* 241.

6 Leviticus 16:5–34.

7 Isaiah 52:11.

8 Edersheim, *The Temple, Its Ministry and Services,* 246–54.

9 Leviticus 16:13.

10 Edersheim, *The Temple, Its Ministry and Services,* 246–54.

11 Isaiah 1:18.

CHAPTER 30

The Day of Atonement and Jesus Christ, the Messiah

Seeing then that we have a great high priest,
that is passed into the heavens, Jesus the Son of God,
let us hold fast our profession. . . .
Let us therefore come boldly unto the throne of grace,
that we may obtain mercy,
and find grace to help in time of need.[1]

IT WAS THE HIGH PRIEST, ALONE, WHO COULD OFFICIATE, AND perform the expiatory services on the Day of Atonement, *Yom Kippur.* It was Jesus Christ, our "great high priest," as Paul calls Him, Who was the only One qualified to perform the sacred act of Atonement for all mankind—and He endured it alone, cut off even from the comforting presence of the Father who loved Him.[2]

Even as the high priest removed his glorious robes to perform his functions on this holy day, Jesus condescended to set aside His power and place in premortality to come to earth for the sake of humanity. Abinadi testified: "Have [the prophets] not said that God himself should come down among the children of men, and take upon him the form of man . . .?"[3] Jesus, our Messiah, set aside the glory He had obtained as one of the Godhead, and condescended to take upon Himself not only mortality, but the suffering, sorrow, and sinful consequences of all mankind.

When Nephi saw the tree of life, and asked to know the interpretation thereof, the first question the angel-guide asked him was if he understood the condescension of God.[4] It is likely that none of us really do!

Gerald N. Lund commented:

Here was Jesus—a member of the Godhead, the Firstborn of the Father, the Creator, Jehovah of the Old Testament—now leaving His divine and holy station; divesting Himself of all that glory and majesty and entering the body of a tiny infant; helpless, completely dependent on His mother and earthly father. That He should not come to the finest of earthly palaces and be . . . showered with jewels but should come to a lowly stable is astonishing. Little wonder that the angel should say to Nephi, "Behold the condescension of God!"[5]

Richard C. Edgley adds:

As the angel taught Nephi, he may have been speaking of two condescensions—one of God the Father and one of the Son, Jesus Christ. . . . While God the Father's condescension reflects His great love for all mankind by permitting His Only Begotten to be sacrificed for even the humblest and lowliest of His children, Christ's condescension was more personal and visible—for He was the sacrifice. His condescension was manifest by who He was and the way He lived. His condescension can be seen in almost every recorded act of His thirty-three years of mortality.[6]

Today, as we appreciate the bright cleanliness of our own temples, it is difficult to imagine the ancient temple with its furnishings covered in blood. The fact that the blood was applied multiple times had to pierce the shell of any distracted or apathetic onlookers. How long would that specific part of the ritual last? It had to take an extended period of time, a period in which each congregant would be forced to consider the sober reality of death and the atoning properties of blood.

With the Fall of Adam and Eve, the Lord instituted the law of sacrifice. Adam and Eve could not escape the painful realization that not only did their transgression separate them from the presence of God, but that they—and all living creatures—now faced physical death. Add to that burden the need to bring about an early death to an innocent animal in order to learn and acknowledge what an atonement meant. While they might have mourned for the animal, what then, of their grief and sorrow in knowing that the premature death and suffering of the Son of God would now be required in order to open the path for their return?[7]

The Lord taught Adam:

That by reason of transgression cometh the fall,
which fall bringeth death,
and inasmuch as ye were born into the world
by water, and blood, and the spirit, which I have made,
and so become of dust a living soul,
even so ye must be born again into the kingdom of heaven,
of water, and of the Spirit, and be cleansed by blood,
even the blood of mine Only Begotten;
that ye might be sanctified from all sin,
and enjoy the words of eternal life in this world,
and eternal life in the world to come,
even immortal glory;
For by the water ye keep the commandment;
by the Spirit ye are justified,
and by the blood ye are sanctified;
. . . And now, behold, I say unto you:
This is the Plan of Salvation unto all men,
through the blood of mine Only Begotten,
who shall come in the meridian of time.[8]

It is the blood of Christ that accesses the mercy of God, just as it is the blood of Christ that activates the grace that enables us to officiate within temple walls. Even as the high priest was instructed to use blood to atone for the unworthiness of himself, the other priests, the congregation, and even the very implements of the temple, Christ's atonement sanctifies and justifies, allowing us entrance to the Father, as illustrated in the Savior's own words:

Listen to him who is the advocate with the Father,
who is pleading your cause before him —
Saying: Father,
behold the sufferings and death of him who did no sin,
in whom thou was well pleased;
behold the blood of thy Son which was shed,
the blood of him whom thou gavest that thyself might be glorified;
Wherefore, Father,
spare these my brethren that believe on my name,
that they may come unto me and have everlasting life.[9]

No wonder John exclaimed: "Jesus Christ . . . him that loved us, and washed us from our sins in his own blood, And hath made us kings and priests unto God and his Father; to him be glory and dominion for ever and ever."[10]

When Moses explained the covenant to the Israelites at Sinai, "he took the book of the covenant, and read in the audience of the people: and they said, All that the Lord hath said will we do, and be obedient. And Moses took the blood, and sprinkled it on the people, and said, Behold the blood of the covenant, which the Lord hath made with you concerning all these words."[11]

That must have been a rather shocking experience, but so necessary to teaching the truth about how important the blood of Jesus Christ would be in sanctifying each one of us. *What would be our reaction today to such a gesture?* King Benjamin's people, filled with the spirit of understanding and a desire to be in a covenant relationship with God, cried out "with one voice, saying, O have mercy, and apply the atoning blood of Christ that we may receive forgiveness of our sins, and our hearts may be purified."[12]

Referring to the ancient temple rituals, Paul taught: "Neither by the blood of goats and calves, but by his own blood he entered in once into the holy place, having obtained eternal redemption for us. For if the blood of bulls and of goats, and the ashes of an heifer sprinkling the unclean, sanctifieth to the purifying of the flesh: How much more shall the blood of Christ, who through the eternal Spirit offered himself without spot to God, purge your conscience from dead works to serve the living God?"[13]

It is clear from ancient ritual and sacrifice, as well as through our sacramental prayers and modern-day scripture, that Jesus Christ *does* want us to have a deep and profound experience as we contemplate His blood shed in our behalf. *We have to take it personally.* His Atonement in our behalf was not a sterile event, but one that caused Him to sweat great drops of blood in Gethsemane, and gush rivers of it as He was scourged by Pilate's soldiers. As the lamb to the slaughter, Jesus was skinned and sacrificed *for us.*

Jesus is also represented in both goats of the *Yom Kippur* ritual. The sins of the people were transferred to the heads of both goats, and the death of the one whose blood was used to sprinkle the mercy seat is an obvious symbol of Christ. However, the scapegoat also represents Christ, as He carries away the burden of the guilt of His people as their sins are carried off and remembered no more.[14] The promise that they can be made as clean as the scarlet ribbon that turned white is conditional upon repentance, as illustrated by King Benjamin's people, who once they cried out for the atoning blood of Christ to be applied to their own lives, "the Spirit of the Lord came upon them, and they were filled with joy, having received a remission of their sins, and having peace of conscience, because of the exceeding faith which they had in Jesus Christ who should come."[15]

At the end of the long day of ceremony, the high priest would bathe once again, and come forth dressed in the golden high-priestly garments that were sometimes referred to as "The Garments of the Bridegroom."[16] As we read in the *High Holiday Prayer Book*, "How radiant was the appearance of the High Priest, when he exited in peace from the holy place! like flashes of light that emanate from the splendor of the angels—such was the appearance of the High Priest."[17] And such *is* the appearance of our High Priest, Jesus Christ, resurrected and glorified, after performing His sacrifice for the children of men.

The fall feasts and festivals were a time for "waking up," for preparation, for repentance, for gathering, and for harvest. We are told that our Bridegroom will come again "soon," and that we should even now be preparing. *What can we learn from the ancient feasts to aid in our preparations?*

Once we have gained some degree of understanding about the feasts and festivals, we will begin to see how often they are referred to throughout scripture, and how reading them in that context can change our perspective dramatically. For example, read Joel, chapter 2, which is about the Second Coming, and see the many allusions to the fall feasts. The first verse begins: "Blow the trumpet in Zion, and sound an alarm in my holy mountain: let all the inhabitants of the land tremble: for the day of the Lord cometh, for it is nigh at hand."[18]

Joel continues with allusions to the Day of Atonement with: "And the Lord shall utter his voice before his army: for his camp is very great: for he is strong that executeth his word: for the day of the Lord is great and very terrible; and who can abide it? Therefore also now, saith the Lord, turn ye even to me with all of your heart, and with fasting, and with weeping, and with mourning: And rend your heart, and not your garments, and turn unto the Lord your God: for he is gracious and merciful, slow to anger, and of great kindness, and repenteth him of the evil."[19]

In the same chapter, Joel prophesies that the Bridegroom will "go forth [out] of His chamber, and the bride [Israel] out of her closet."[20] Continuing in the imagery of the feast symbolism, Joel sees the great harvest of souls that will occur after the Lord recovers and gathers together the remnant of His people.[21] This great harvest is symbolized in "The Last, Great Feast," known as *Sukkot*, or Feast of Tabernacles, when all is safely gathered in, and the Lord will dwell with His people in peace and rejoicing.

The feasts and festivals of the Messiah help us to *remember*. Through them, we remember the covenants which have been made with our fathers, through them we find hope for the future, and through them, we find the Messiah, who is Jehovah, Yeshua, or Jesus Christ.

---

1 Hebrews 4:14, 16.

2 Matthew 27:46.

3 Mosiah 13:34.

4 1 Nephi 11:16.

5 Lund, *Jesus Christ: Key to the Plan of Salvation*, 16.

6 Edgley, "The Condescension of God," *Ensign,* Dec. 2001.

7 See Moses 5:5–10.

8 Moses 6:59–60, 62.

9 Doctrine and Covenants 45:3–5.

10 Revelation 1:5–6.

11 Exodus 24:7–8.

12 Mosiah 4:2.

13 Hebrews 9:12–14.

14 Doctrine and Covenants 58:42.

15 Mosiah 4:3.

16 See "Priesthood, Part 1: The Garments of the Priesthood," judeochristianclarion.com/teaching-letters/garments-of-priesthood/.

17 Silverman, *High Holiday Prayer Book*.

18 Joel 2:1.

19 Joel 2:11–13.

20 Joel 2:16.

21 Joel 2:16, 19, 22–26, 32.

—⌒⊙⌒—

CHAPTER 31

The Day of Atonement, *Yom Kippur*, Work Chart

By now, you have come to realize that each symbol can evoke multiple meanings and applications to your own personal life. In this case, none of the application forms are pre-filled for this most holy day of the year. Please take some time to ponder and consider what applications are pertinent to your understanding and life today.

The Day of Atonement—*Yom Kippur*

Symbol	Christ	Personal Insight/ Application
Shofar calls		
A Day of Fasting and Prayer		
Assignment to Life or Death "sealed"		

Symbol	Christ	Personal Insight/ Application
The whole congregation assembles at the temple		
High Priest performs all the duties and sacrifices		
High Priest divests himself of his golden garments		
First expiation done for the High Priest and his family		
Two goats chosen—one for Jehovah and one as a scapegoat		
Smoke and incense burned in the Holy of Holies		
Blood of the bullock sprinkled on Mercy Seat of the Ark of the Covenant		

Symbol	Christ	Personal Insight/ Application
Blood of the goat sprinkled on Mercy Seat of the Ark of the Covenant		
Blood of the bullock and of the goat mixed and sprinkled on Altar of Incense		
Scarlet cloths on the goats—on the horn of the scapegoat, the throat of the goat for Jehovah		
Scapegoat sent into the wilderness		
Scarlet cloth tied to temple door— turns white		

CHAPTER 32

─── ∽◎⌒ ───

Feast of Tabernacles, *Sukkot*

And it shall come to pass,
that every one that is left of all the nations
which came against Jerusalem
shall even go up from year to year to worship the King,
the Lord of hosts, and to keep the feast of tabernacles.[1]

THE FEAST OF TABERNACLES, OR *SUKKOT*, WAS THE GREAT AND final culmination of the three fall feasts. These began with The Feast of Trumpets, or Rosh *Hoshanah*, which included a ten-day period of reflection and repentance that led to The Day of Atonement, or *Yom Kippur*. The Feast of Tabernacles, or *Sukkot*, occurred five days following The Day of Atonement, and lasted for seven days, with an occasional "octave," or eighth day, to the feast depending upon where the Sabbath fell in that year. These three feasts were together considered the holiest days of the year, and took place in the seventh month of *Tishri* of the Israelite calendar. The temple was the center of the celebrations, with rituals taking place at various times throughout the day.

The Feast of Tabernacles was a feast of celebration and joy, a time of harvest, and a time of remembrance of the Lord's care for the children of Israel. It is referred to as "The Time of Our Joy," and gets its name from the temporary "booths or tabernacles" (*sukkot*) constructed for the people to live in on the streets, on their rooftops, or on their porches for the seven days' duration of the feast. The booths were to be formed with "leafy" branches, symbolizing life and fruitfulness, and were a reminder that the children of Israel had once lived in temporary tents and dwellings after their escape from Egypt. The

Lord had provided for them in miraculous ways: manna and quail from heaven, the presence of His glory in the tabernacle, protection from their enemies, and clothing that did not wear out. Families were given instruction that they were to eat their meals in the *sukkah*, share stories of Israel's redemption, make music, and invite friends over to join in the celebrations. They were also to sleep in the *sukkah* for the seven nights of the festival.

The *sukkah* was also a symbol of faith that the Lord would once again—and always—provide for His people, and that one day they would live with Him in His home, or kingdom, forever.

With this hope in mind, the temporary booths are sometimes referred to as the "House of HaShem" (The House of the Lord, The House of God).[2] This, of course, is the same name given to the ancient tabernacle, and later, to the temple. It is a hopeful promise that each individual and family would enjoy a communion-type relationship with the Lord in the Messianic age.

The Temple Institute in Jerusalem has earnestly sought to restore the heart and soul of ancient temple practices, and to prepare for a future temple to be built again on the temple mount. They contributed the following insight into the purpose of the *sukkah*, and its message of love and mercy:

> And lest one feel dejected, despondent or fearful that perhaps his judgment was not favorable, and he has lost that Divine connection— immediately after the Day of Atonement he is given bundles of commandments to fulfill, the construction of the booth and the preparation of the four species. Then he goes out into the booth itself, symbol of Divine mercy; instead of running away from the Holy One he flees directly into His presence, as it were. There, he is overwhelmed by the realization of the depth of God's love and concern.[3]

What a beautiful image to relate to our own experience in temples today! While the need for a temple recommend invites us to consider our standing before God, and the need to be clean and repentant, that opportunity for contemplation sometimes makes us wonder about our own worthiness and whether we will be accepted by God. If we followed the example of the teaching above, we would run directly towards the presence of God in His temple, realizing, and cherishing, the depth of His love and concern for us as His children.

What could be gained in following the pattern of the fall feasts, and planning a specified period during which we remove ourselves from the burdens of everyday life, study the scriptures, contemplate our relationship with the Lord, and spend seven days going to the temple, remembering His care of us, and renewing our covenants with Him?

The Feast of Tabernacles is an opportunity to express gratitude for God's care in the past, and thanksgiving for the season's harvest, but it is also a looking *forward* to the coming (first and second) of the Messiah. The *sukkah's* rooftop is deliberately left with large openings between the branches, so that the inhabitants can watch the heavens for the signs of the coming Lord.

The Lord had given instructions regarding the feast days from Sinai, and the rituals that accompanied the holy days were teaching tools to instruct and prepare the people for their unique role as Israelites, but also to help them to know and recognize their God. Just as the "booths" reminded them of what the Lord had already done for them, other aspects of the celebrations foretold of the mission and atonement of the Messiah. It also foreshadowed the gathering of Israel, the grafting in of the Gentiles, and the Millennial Day with its prophesied "Feast of the Bridegroom," or "Marriage Supper of the Lamb."[4]

During the week-long celebrations, worshippers carried *lulav* from four species of plant life (myrtle, palm, and willow branches combined with citrus fruit), in their hands as they made their way daily to the temple. These different varieties of vegetation were to remind the Israelites of what they had seen as they journeyed to the promised land, and of the fruit that was growing there when they arrived. But, in view of the other practices of the Feast, the four species may also symbolize the different varieties of people from all parts of the world that would join in the covenant family of Israel.

The teachers of the day reminded the people that many of the symbols of the Feast had to do with harvesting souls, particularly the commission to sow and harvest amongst the Gentiles.

Seventy bullocks were sacrificed to represent the seventy nations of the world, and many looked to Zechariah's prophecy that the Gentiles would eventually join in keeping the Feast of Tabernacles: "And it shall come to pass, that every one that is left of all the nations which came against Jerusalem shall even go up from year to year to worship the King, the Lord of hosts, and to keep the feast of tabernacles."[5]

Enormous candelabra were set up on each corner of the temple mount, each approximately 75 feet in height. Each candelabra stand had four golden cups filled with oil, and wicks made from priests' worn-out clothing. The light shone forth from the temple, and flooded the surrounding hillsides and homes, lighting the entire city, reminiscent of the glorious days when the *Shechinah,* or glory of the Lord, filled the Lord's Holy House. This glorious light was meant to draw all people of all nations to the temple, where they would hear the word of the Lord. The lighting of the candelabra, together with the outpouring of the water from the Pool of Siloam were the highlights of the temple festivities, and occurred on all but the last day of the Feast.

As dawn came each day, and the lights from the candelabra were extinguished, a concourse of Levites marched in solemn procession from the top of the center court of the temple, sounding their trumpets as they descended the fifteen steps down to the Court of the Women, and on to the Beautiful Gate to the east. Still sounding their trumpets, they turned round and faced westward to the Holy Place, and together they chanted: "Our fathers, who were in this place, they turned their backs on the Sanctuary of Jehovah, and their faces eastward, for they worshipped eastward, the sun; but we, our eyes are towards Jehovah. We are Jehovah's—our eyes are towards Jehovah."[6] It must have been a stirring sight!

The Festival was distinctive for its rituals. One, accompanied by fanfare and crowds, was the water libation, or "outpouring of water." As the morning sacrifices were being examined and prepared, a priest, accompanied by a joyous procession with music, went down to the Pool of Siloam (*Shiloach*), from which he drew water into a golden pitcher. At the same time that he and his followers went to the Pool, another group of priests went to the Kidron Valley to collect fresh willow branches, up to 16 feet tall, which, amidst the blasts of the priests' trumpets, they mounted on either side of the altar of burnt-offering.[7] Smaller branches were distributed among the people in the courtyard.

The priest from Siloam would time his arrival to coincide exactly with the time that his priestly brethren carried up the pieces of the sacrifice to lay on the altar. He was greeted by another three-fold blast of the trumpet, as he mounted the stairs and positioned himself next to the altar. Yet another priest stepped forward with *his* offering: a flagon of wine. The priest with the water and the priest with the wine poured into their respective silver basins; one on the eastern side of the altar (the wine), and the other on the west. All was done with perfect exactness: the final drops of water were to coincide with those of the wine. As the water and wine were poured, the people waved their branches towards the altar, shouting *Ana Hashem Hoshiya Na* ("Please, Lord, save us!") from the *Hallel.*[8] On the seventh day of the Feast, the people circled the altar seven times, waving their willows, repeating "Save now, we beseech thee," seven times.[9]

As part of the Feast of Tabernacles, every seven years, or as circumstances demanded, a *Hak'hel* ceremony would be held. The ceremony required all Israelites and non-Israelites who lived amongst them to assemble at the temple, to hear from the king. The king was to give a report of his stewardship before God, read from the Torah (or scriptures), call the people to repent, and to renew their covenants with God. A special tower was built so that all could see and hear the king clearly. The practice was taken from this instruction in Deuteronomy:

> *Moses wrote this law, and delivered it unto the priests . . .*
> *and unto all the elders of Israel.*
> *And Moses commanded them, saying,*
> *At the end of every seven years,*
> *in the solemnity of the year of*
> *release, in the feast of tabernacles,*
> *When all Israel is come to appear before the Lord thy God*
> *in the place which he shall choose [the temple in Jerusalem],*
> *thou shalt read this law before all Israel in their hearing.*
> *Gather the people together, men, and women, and children,*
> *and thy stranger that is within thy gates, that they may hear,*
> *and that they may learn, and fear the Lord your God,*
> *and observe to do all the words of this law:*
> *And that their children, which have not known any thing,*
> *may hear, and learn to fear the Lord your God.*[10]

John A. Tvedtnes wrote:

The gathering together of the people at the Feast of Tabernacles provided the backdrop for several special ceremonies in ancient Israel, including (a) thanksgiving for the fall harvest, (b) prayers for rain to begin the new agricultural year, (c) a rehearsal of the law of God and a public commitment to obey his commandments, (d) coronation of a new king or a renewal of the kingship, (e) celebration of the end of the season of war (due to rainy weather) and the establishment of peace, and (f) dedication of the temple. In the third year, tithes of farm produce were collected for the Levites and the poor,[11] with a call for special help to the poor during the seventh year.[12]

Tvedtnes explains that successive Tabernacles feasts held the the same principle elements:

1. A recital of *God's dealings with Israel* during the exodus.[13]
2. *Reading from the Law.*[14]
3. An exhortation to *teach the Law to subsequent generations.*[15]
4. Recalling the *covenant and assembly* at Sinai,[16] including (a) a *recitation of the law,*[17] *(b)* a reminder of the Exodus from Egypt,[18] (c) a threat that if the people break the covenant, they will be *driven from the promised land,*[19] while if they keep the commandments *their days will be prolonged therein,*[20] and (d) mention of the *law being written on tablets of stone.*[21] Many of these features are repeated in Moses' exhortation.
5. Heaven and earth are called to witness the pronouncing *curses for disobedience.*[22]
6. A promise of *prosperity and long life* for obedience to the Law.[23]
7. The people being sent back to their *tents.*[24]
8. The conclusion, or *Shema,*[25] which teaches that (a) *God must be loved and honored,*[26] (a) *children should be taught the Law,*[27] (c) the law should be *written down,* and (d) that God will reward obedience by *prosperity.*[28,]

An *Ensign* article states that:

Twelve researchers have collaborated in a detailed comparison of King Benjamin's speech with ancient Jewish festivals. The similarities are astonishing—hundreds of phrases and incidents recorded in the speech echo those in three Jewish festivals. Jewish festivals, for instance, began with a traditional prayer called the *Shecheheyanu.*

It opened, "Lord God, king of the universe, who has *kept us and preserved us* to reach this season. . . ." King Benjamin echoed those words, "to that God who has . . . *kept and preserved you . . .* that ye may live," pointing out how no one could really be a profitable servant of God." [29]

King Benjamin of Zarahemla was not the only Israelite king to perform the *Hak'hel* ceremony for *Sukkot* or Feast of Tabernacles rituals. Most scholars agree that when King Josiah of Jerusalem stood in front of the pillar of the temple and led his people in making a most solemn covenant, he was likely following the Feast's customs.[30] This was the most solemn duty of the king, who was "only acting in the service of God."[31]

Stephen D. Ricks wrote:

The king in Israel had an added responsibility of acting as guardian of the covenant between the Lord and his people—a concept that seems to have no parallel among neighboring peoples. He was expected to be an obedient follower of God and to lead his people in obeying this covenant. As guardian of the covenant and of the law, the Israelite king took special measures in his capacity of teacher of the torah, being the highest responsible authority in all matters appertaining to the department of the law.[32]

But, not all of the kings of Israel kept the sacred feast days, or honored God, as had been commanded at Sinai. Scriptural records seem to indicate that when there was not a righteous king to lead the *Hak'hel*, the Lord called other emissaries to do so. Ezra the priest conducted it after the Jews' return from Babylon,[33] and certain accounts indicate that Jeremiah may also have performed the ceremony as commanded by the Lord just prior to the Babylonian conquest of Jerusalem.[34]

It is of note that King Solomon dedicated the first Jerusalem temple on the Feast of Tabernacles.[35]

1 Zechariah 14:16.

2 Rabbi Yitzchak Reuven, Email message to author, Sept. 26, 2007.

3 Email message to author from Temple Institute, templeinstitute.org.

4 Revelation 19:7.

5 Zechariah 14:16; Edersheim, *The Temple: Its Ministry and Services,* 219.

6 Edersheim, *The Life and Times of Jesus the Messiah,* 577.

7 "Three Mitzvot," *Temple Institute,* templeinstitute.org, sukkot-part-3.

8 Edersheim, *The Temple: Its Ministry and Services,* 220.

9 Chumney, *The Seven Festivals of the Messiah,* 174.

10 Deuteronomy 31:9–1.

11 Deuteronomy 14:27–29; 26:11–14; Amos 4:4.

12 Deuteronomy 15:7–11; Tvedtnes, "King Benjamin and the Feast of Tabernacles," *Maxwell Institute.*

13 Deuteronomy 1:6–3, 29; 5:6.

14 Deuteronomy 4:1–9, 11–25; 5:6–21.

15 Deuteronomy 4:9–10.

16 Deuteronomy 4:10–13, 36; 5:1–5, 22–31.

17 Deuteronomy 4:14–19.

18 Deuteronomy 4:20, 34, 37–38.

19 Deuteronomy 4:25–27.

20 Deuteronomy 4:40, 5:31–33.

21 Deuteronomy 5:22.

22 Deuteronomy 4:26–39.

23 Deuteronomy 4:40; 5:32–6:3.

24 Deuteronomy 5:30.

25 Deuteronomy 6:4–10.

26 Deuteronomy 6:5.

27 Deuteronomy 6:7.

28 Deuteronomy 6:10–11; Tvedtnes, "King Benjamin and the Feast of Tabernacles," *Maxwell Institute.*

29 "Research and Perspectives: Recent Studies on the Book of Mormon," *Ensign,* June 1989.

30 2 Kings 23.

31 Mosiah 2:17.

32 Ricks, "Kingship, Coronation, and Covenant in Mosiah 1-6," *King Benjamin's Speech: "That Ye May Learn Wisdom.*

33 Ezra 10:1–10.

34 Jeremiah 7:1–2; See Jeremiah 2, 3, 6–7.

35 1 Kings 8.

CHAPTER 33

—⸺⊂∞⊃⸺—

Jesus at the Feast of Tabernacles

As has been established, Jesus and His apostles kept the feasts in Jerusalem, and much of Jesus's public ministry was recorded as taking place during those feast days. He would have had a wide-ranging audience, as Israelite men throughout the mid-eastern world would travel to Jerusalem in order to comply with the commandment to present themselves at the temple before the Lord.

On one notable occasion of the Feast of Tabernacles, Jesus did not go to Jerusalem openly, nor did He attend the first days of the celebration. He knew that there were many who sought to kill Him, and He knew that His time to die had not yet come. His half-brothers had mockingly challenged Him to leave Galilee and go to the Feast, and there "show himself to the world," for John tells us, his brethren did not believe in Him.[1] Their challenge to Him to go and "show Himself" was painfully ironic, for every ritual performed at the Feast testified of, and demonstrated that Jesus was the Messiah they had been waiting for. He, Jesus Christ, was Jehovah, Who they worshipped through their celebrations. It was *He* who had led and protected them during the long journey between Egypt and their Promised Land, it was *He* who had provided the manna, and it was *He* who had shown His glorious presence in the Tabernacle.

The Levite priests had made their procession to the Beautiful Gate—the same Gate through which Jesus would enter His last week of mortality and make His "triumphal entry" into Jerusalem, and also the same Gate by which He *will* enter when He comes again to rule.[2] It was the Gate reserved for Kings and for the Messiah.[3] They turned from that Gate toward the Holy Place and chanted that they would never turn their backs on Jehovah as their ancestors had done, yet when Jesus taught in the temple, the priests and leaders of the people were the first to accuse and question Him.

"How knoweth this man letters, having never learned?" they asked, referring to the fact that He had not attended any of *their* Rabbinical schools.[4] When some said that He must surely be the Christ, they responded quickly: "Howbeit we know this man whence he is: but when Christ cometh, no man knoweth whence he is. Shall Christ come out of Galilee? Hath not the scripture said, That Christ cometh of the seed of David, and out of the town of Bethlehem, where David was?"[5]

They thought of Jesus merely as a "Nazarene, a Galilean," having no idea, and seemingly no desire to check into the fact that He *was* born of David, and *in Bethlehem*! Jesus cried out to them: "Ye both know me, and ye know whence I am: and I am not come of myself, but he that sent me is true, whom ye know not."[6]

They were so angry at Him that they sent temple guards to arrest Him, but even the soldiers stayed to listen to Him, and returned to their captains empty- handed, saying, amazed: "Never man spake like this man."[7]

The seventh day of the Feast was the only day on which the water-pouring ceremony was not performed. It was on this day that Jesus stood in the temple and said:

> If any man thirst, let him come unto me, and drink.
> He that believeth on me, as the scripture hath said,
> out of his belly shall flow rivers of living water.[8]

The people associated the water-pouring ceremony with the prophecy of Isaiah: "Therefore with joy shall ye draw water out of the wells of salvation."[9] The pool of Siloam carried the same root-name as *Shilo*, or *Shiloah*, one of the names of the longed-for Messiah, Who would bring the very salvation they craved. Isaiah, to whom they so often looked for hope of the coming Messiah, had prophesied concerning the waters of salvation, and had also warned the people that they must not "refuse the waters of Shiloah that go softly."[10] Now, they were in danger of doing exactly that, as they stubbornly refused to acknowledge Jesus's bold claims. Everything testified of Jesus as the Messiah:

the pool of Siloam streamed forth from a rock which had been named "The Virgin's Fountain" by the people.[11] Now, the Virgin's Son stood before them, offering them the waters of life, even as He had already shared that testimony with the woman of Samaria:

> *Whosoever drinketh of the water that I shall give him*
> *shall never thirst;*
> *but the water that I shall give him*
> *shall be in him a well of water*
> *springing up into everlasting life.*[12]

The water for the water-pouring ceremony was drawn from the pool of Siloam, and poured on the western side of the altar. At the same time, wine was poured on the eastern side of the altar—the side facing the Mount of Olives, and Gethsemane. When the Roman soldier pierced Jesus's side, both water and blood flowed out, which physicians believe was a result of a broken heart.[13] Wine is frequently associated with blood, as with the institution of the sacrament.

Jesus's first recorded miracle was turning water that was used for purification into wine—and not just any wine—but the best wine of the wedding supper.[14] Some have felt that in turning the water that the Jews used to cleanse their hands into wine, Jesus was foreshadowing the truth that no amount of "rule-following" could actually cleanse their hearts, but only the "best blood" shed in sacrifice, and partaken of in covenant could accomplish the healing and cleansing of the nation. The reliance of the Israelites on their strict adherence to the Law could not save them; they had to understand and embrace the *spirit* of the Law.

Many rabbis taught that the pouring out of the water was associated with the pouring out of the Holy Spirit. The Temple Institute teaches, "Herein lies the true secret of the festival of the water libation: the great joy was in the receiving of prophetic inspiration."[15] Jesus told Nicodemus that a man must be born of the water and the spirit in order to enter into the kingdom of God,[16] thus linking the two, even as they are linked in the rabbinic teachings. Jesus promised that the water He could provide would be a "well springing up," a constant supply. To those in the mideast, who depended so much on the spring and fall rains, the promise of water would hold great hope—and Jesus was promising that it would always be available as needed, without running out.

Ezekiel saw a day when water would flow forth from the temple in Jerusalem, and heal the dead sea. He saw that those waters brought life to everything they encountered:

> *And it shall come to pass, that everything that liveth,*
> *which moveth, whithersoever the rivers shall come,*
> *shall live.*[17]

While those healing waters present an image of what will actually and literally transpire, they also have a symbolic meaning. If they are, in fact, associated with the outpouring of the Holy Ghost, then they can be life-giving indeed. It is the Holy Ghost who testifies and teaches us truth about God, about ourselves, and about our relationship to others. The Holy Ghost can produce constant truth and direction, even as a fresh-water fountain that never runs dry. As the Spirit testifies to us of the Plan of Salvation—the very salvation the water libation represented—we can receive not only joy, but genuine healing. It is the Holy Ghost that gives answer to our prayers.

The priests and the people gathered their branches for the ceremonies by crossing the Kidron Valley—the same valley Jesus crossed when He went from Jerusalem to the Garden of Gethsemane. Perhaps their palms came from the very trees in that garden. They waved them towards the altar, upon which the sacrifice lay, shouting "Hosanna! Save us now, Jehovah," the same phrase they shouted nearly six months later as He made His way through the streets on the great day known as the Triumphal Entry, as they waved palms in their hands.

The priests had assembled the giant willow branches on each side of the altar, which some have come to view as a symbol of the cross, or tree, upon which Jesus would offer His last sacrifice.

How did Jesus feel, watching His people going through all the motions, and saying all the right words, but totally missing the meaning? Well had He said: "This people draweth nigh unto me with their mouth, and honoureth me with their lips; but their heart is far from me!"[18] *Might we also be in danger of the same blindness?*

It may have been at the very moment that the great candelabra were being lit, their golden cups filled with up to seven gallons of olive oil, that He declared:

I am the light of the world:
he that followeth me shall not walk in darkness,
but shall have the light of life.[19]

The candelabra shed light over the entire city, and represented the light of the word of Jehovah going out to all the world. Jesus *is* Jehovah—He who gave the Law, and met with Moses from within the Holy of Holies, and presented the rituals of the temple so that His people could come to know Him, and find healing truth. The olive oil within the lamp-stands undoubtedly came from the olive press in Gethsemane, just across the valley, yet another symbol of His anointing and His sacrifice (*Gethsemane* means "olive press"—His blood was *pressed* out of every pore).

When Jesus gave the Nephites the charge to be the "light of the world," He clarified:

Therefore, hold up your light that it may shine unto the world.
Behold I am the light which ye shall hold up.[20]

The best that we can do is to *reflect* His light to others, and bring them to its source. And, in order to do so, we must be *filled* with His Spirit. All of these truths are symbolized in the rituals of the Feast of Tabernacles.

The Pharisees' response to Jesus was: "You bear record of yourself; therefore your witness is not true."[21] Jesus replied: "The Father that sent me beareth witness of me. . . . Ye neither know me, nor my Father: if ye had known me, ye should have known my Father also. . . . I have many things to say and to judge of you: but he that sent me is true; and I speak to the world those things which I have heard of him. . . . When ye have lifted up the Son of Man, then shall ye know that I am he, and that I do nothing of myself; but as my Father hath taught me, I speak these things. And he that sent me is with me: the Father hath not left me alone; for I do always those things that please him."[22] As He stood in the temple court, with the trees assembled against the altar of sacrifice, Jesus *told* the Pharisees the method by which He would die: "When ye have lifted up the Son of Man, then shall ye know that I am he."[23]

"Why do ye not understand my speech?" He questioned, and then He provided the answer: "Even because ye cannot bear my word."[24]

Can we "bear" the word of Christ? Do we seek His light?

Jesus made a pertinent statement in our day and dispensation: "They who are not chosen have sinned a very grievous sin, in that they are walking in darkness at noon-day."[25] The people who stood in Jesus's presence at the Feast of Tabernacles had the brightness of noon-day before them, but they closed their eyes, and missed the healing power that comes from the Light of Christ.

Although we do not keep the Feast of Tabernacles, we, too, are surrounded by symbols and witnesses of Christ. Alma testified that "all things denote there is a God; yea, even the earth, and all things that are upon the face of it, yea, and its motion, yea, and also all the planets which move in their regular form do witness that there is a Supreme Creator."[26]

There is a prophecy of another great day to come; when all people will know Jehovah as Jesus Christ and perform the same joyful salute as that performed during the Feast of Tabernacles.

John wrote:

I beheld, and, lo, a great multitude,
which no man could number, of all nations, and kindreds,
and people, and tongues,
stood before the throne, and before the Lamb,
clothed with white robes, and palms in their hands;
And cried with a loud voice, saying,
Salvation to our God which sitteth upon the throne,
and unto the Lamb."[27]

All who wave their palms in *that* day will finally understand and rejoice in who Jesus is!

We have the opportunity to prepare now for that day when we participate in the Hosanna Shout at the dedication of temples and other special events, such as Easter 2020 (3 days short of Passover) at General Conference, under the direction of President Russell M. Nelson.

Hosanna, Hosanna, Hosanna to God and the Lamb!

May we all praise the Lamb of God, who takes away the sins of the world, and offers salvation to every creature . . . and, as the Primary children sing, may we "gladly, gladly, walk in the Light."[28]

1 John 7:1–8

2 See Ezekiel 43:4, 44:1–2.

3 1 Chronicles 9:18.

4 John 7:15.

5 John 7:27, 41–42.

6 John 7:28.

7 John 7:32, 45–46.

8 John 7:37–38.

9 Isaiah 12:3.

10 Isaiah 8:6.

11 Talmage, *Jesus the Christ*, 392.

12 John 4:14.

13 Talmage, *Jesus the Christ*, 620; Lund, "What the Atoning Sacrifice Meant for Jesus."

14 John 2:1–11.

15 *"The Festival of Sukkot in the Holy Temple,"* templeinstitute.org.

16 John 3:5.

17 Ezekiel 47:9.

18 Matthew 15:8; Isaiah 29:13.

19 John 8:12.

20 3 Nephi 18:24.

21 John 8:13.

22 John 8:18–19, 26–29.

23 John 8:28.

24 John 8:43, Joseph Smith Translation.

25 Doctrine and Covenants 95:6.

26 Alma 30:44.

27 Revelation 7:9–10.

28 "Teach Me to Walk in the Light," *Hymns*, no. 304.

CHAPTER 34

───⌒⊙⌒───

The Final Harvest, The Gathering of Israel

Therefore, behold, the days come, saith the Lord,
that they shall no more say, The Lord liveth,
which brought up the children of Israel
out of the land of Egypt;
But, the Lord liveth,
which brought up and which led the seed of the house of Israel
out of the north country,
and from all countries whither I had driven them;
and they shall dwell in their own land. . . .
For, lo, the days come, saith the Lord,
that I will bring again the captivity of my people
Israel and Judah, saith the Lord:
and I will cause them to return to the land
that I gave to their fathers, and they shall possess it.[1]

THE DELIVERANCE OF ISRAEL FROM BONDAGE IN EGYPT HAS LONG been viewed as one of the greatest miracles performed by God in behalf of His people. But, Jeremiah prophesied that in the last days people would no longer speak of the escape from Egypt as the greatest miracle, but would declare that His greatest miracle would be the reclamation of Israel, and the gathering of the various tribes scattered and lost throughout the vineyards of the world.[2]

Jeremiah's prophecy of gathering still has facets yet to be fulfilled; the prophecy does not pertain only to the Jews' return to Jerusalem from Babylon. The prophecy distinctly mentions both Israel and

Judah. While the Jews have, for the most part, kept their distinct tribal identity, Israel has not, and has yet to be gathered home. In addition, while there has been a partial return of the Jews to their homeland—both following the Babylonian captivity, and after World War II—there are yet to be many more gathered to Jerusalem.

The Feast of Tabernacles celebrated the last harvest of the agricultural year, and foreshadowed the final harvest of souls. Many symbols pointed to the grafting in of the Gentiles to the covenant family of Israel, including the sacrifice of the seventy bullocks for the seventy nations, the four species of plant carried each day by the celebrants, and the earlier reading and lauding of Ruth, a Gentile who married Boaz of Judah.

The final gathering of Israel requires a unique relationship between the literal family of Israel and the Gentiles, who like Ruth, have chosen to make Israel's God their God. It's important to recognize that the family of Israel is more than a specific bloodline. *All* people are invited to become a part of Israel as they accept Jesus Christ as the Messiah, and enter into The New and Everlasting Covenant. Israel is the name of God's covenant family, and all people from all races are invited to belong to it.

The Apostle Paul taught:

> *For ye are all the children of God by faith in Christ Jesus . . .*
> *There is neither Jew nor Gentile,*
> *there is neither bond nor free,*
> *there is neither male nor female:*
> *for ye are all one in Christ Jesus. And if ye be Christ's,*
> *then are ye Abraham's seed, and heirs according to the promise.*[3]

The prophet Nephi added:

> *. . . and he inviteth them all to come unto him and partake of his*
> *goodness; and he denieth none that come unto him,*
> *black and white, bond and free, male and female . . .*
> *and all are alike unto God, both Jew and Gentile.*[4]

The unique and vital relationship between Israel and the Gentiles is complex and beautiful. If understood properly, it brings life and healing to each group.

The "Jews"—those from the tribe of Judah—are, for the most part, the only remaining tribe of Israel who have retained their identity. Through the Jews, we have the Bible, the Law, the original record of God's dealings with His people, the prophecies concerning the Plan of Salvation and the Messiah, and the covenant. Jesus is from the tribe of Judah, and a Jew. Blessed be the Jews for their careful preservation of that which is sacred and holy!

When the Gentiles accept the fulness of the Gospel, their hearts must, of necessity, be filled with love and gratitude for the Jews for preserving the truths that lead to salvation. In fact, Joseph Smith's prayer on the first temple of this dispensation (Kirtland Temple, March 1836), included a plea in behalf of all of the tribes of Israel, and for the Jews, specifically:

> *But thou knowest that thou hast a great love for the children of Jacob, who*
> *have been scattered upon the mountains for a long time,*
> *in a cloudy and dark day.*
> *We therefore ask thee to have mercy upon the children of Jacob,*
> *that Jerusalem, from this hour, may begin to be redeemed;*
> *And the yoke of bondage may begin to be broken off from the house of David;*
> *And the children of Judah may begin to return to the lands*
> *which thou didst give to Abraham, their father.*[5]

At another temple dedication—the first temple in Jerusalem— King Solomon, David's son, and a descendant of Judah, foresaw a Gentile helping his people. Solomon prayed:

> *Moreover concerning a stranger,*
> *that is not of thy people Israel,*
> *but cometh out of a far country for thy name's sake;*
> *. . . when he shall come and pray toward this house;*
> *Hear thou in heaven thy dwelling place,*
> *and do according to all that the stranger calleth to thee for:*
> *that all the people of the earth may know thy name,*
> *to fear thee, as do thy people Israel;*
> *and that they may know that this house,*
> *which I have builded, is called by thy name.*[6]

Solomon dedicated the Jerusalem Temple on the Feast of Tabernacles, a Feast that came to have special significance in recognizing that the Gentiles would become a part of the Israelite family and the harvest of souls. Thousands of years after Solomon's plea that the Lord would listen to a Gentile's prayer in behalf of his people, Orson Hyde, an apostle of this dispensation, stood facing the Holy Mount in Jerusalem and pled in behalf of the Israelites and the Jews. On October 24, 1841, Orson Hyde ascended the Mount of Olives, built an altar to the Lord, and offered this prayer (in part):

Thy servant . . . has safely arrived in this place
to dedicate and consecrate this land unto Thee,
for the gathering together of Judah's scattered remnants
according to the predictions of the holy Prophets—
for the building up of Jerusalem again
after it has been trodden down by the Gentiles so long,
and for *rearing a Temple* in honor of Thy name . . .
Let them know that it is
Thy good pleasure to restore the kingdom unto Israel—
raise up Jerusalem as its capital,
and *constitute her people a distinct nation and government,*
with David Thy servant,
even a descendant from the loins of ancient David to be their king.[7]

The dedicatory prayers on these two temples—the first temple in Jerusalem, and the first temple in the latter-days—illustrate the profound brotherhood between the family of Israel and the Gentiles.

Many of the Gentiles joining The Church of Jesus Christ of Latter-day Saints are discovering through their patriarchal-blessing revelation that they are actually descendants from the lost tribes of Israel. When the ten tribes were carried away by Assyria, they were assimilated into the culture of the countries where they were taken captive. Most lost their identity as Israel, yet the Lord remembered them, and remembered His covenant with Abraham that He would remember His seed forever,[8] and that through Abraham's seed, all the nations of the world would be blessed "even with the blessings of the Gospel, which are the blessings of salvation, even of life eternal."[9]

Isaiah illustrated the symbiotic relationship between the Gentiles and Israel in the following prophecy:

> *Thus saith the Lord God,*
> *Behold, I will lift up mine hand to the Gentiles,*
> *and set up my standard to the people:*
> *and they shall bring thy sons in their arms,*
> *and thy daughters shall be carried upon their shoulders.*
> *And kings shall be thy nursing fathers,*
> *and their queens thy nursing mothers:*
> *they shall bow down to thee with their face toward the earth,*
> *and lick up the dust of thy feet;*
> *and thou shalt know that I am the Lord;*
> *for they shall not be ashamed that wait for me.*[10]

In this prophecy, the Gentiles assist Israel in carrying them home, and restoring them to their lands (and their covenants), but the Gentile "kings and queens" bow down to the Israelites as well. In a figurative sense, the Gentiles have become "kings and queens" because of their adoption into the covenant, which promises a holy nation, and a kingdom of priests (and priestesses).[11] John also rejoices in the fact that Jesus makes us kings and priests (and queens and priestesses) unto God in the book of Revelation.[12] Isaiah makes it clear that the Gentiles and the Israelites *need each other* in order to reach their full potential.

Considering that many who are called Gentiles are actually from one of the lost tribes of Israel, it is interesting to note that a group of rabbis wrote a letter called "Epistle to the Ten Tribes" in 1830 in Jerusalem. Led by Rabbi Israel ben Shmuel Ashkenazi of Shklov, the rabbis came to believe, based on a reading of the *Zohar,* that a reunion between the lost ten tribes of Israel and the children of Judah was necessary before the Messiah would come and redeem His people.

Rabbi Israel believed that the ten tribes held certain keys to the redemption and restoration of Judah, the holy lands and the temple. He wrote that there would be a certain order that would occur in that redemption, and felt that anything taken out of order would corrupt the whole process. In other words, in his mind, Jerusalem would not be rebuilt until after the gathering and unification of the tribes began, and proper judges, counselors, or those who "ordained" by authority were called to lead them.

Most interesting to the Latter-day Saint scholar, would be Rabbi Israel's reliance on a teaching by Maimonides that the "renewal of ordination was a necessary precondition to the Messiah's advent," and that this ordination would "establish an authorized court of ordained sages" or judges.[13]

Maimonides taught that as the Jews did not have this proper ordination, the ten tribes must have a leader amongst them who possessed the ordination, or authority, and could thereby ordain others to sit in the councils of judges.[14] Arie Morgenstern explains:

> This was the first time in the history of Jewish messianism that there was an effort to assign the Ten Tribes a central role in the redemptive process through renewal of ordination. The Ten Tribes had always been taken into account, particularly during times of messianic awakening, but only insofar as it was believed that they would be discovered at the end of days and might bring their military prowess to bear against the enemies of the Jews. Never before had they been seen as those who would renew ordination.[15]

The first part of the letter reads:

> First, we plead with you on behalf of the entire congregation of Israel, whose dignity has been trampled upon, and his holy name which has become deserted, as we are asked "where is your God?" our energy are depleted and our minds clouded and have not the strength to pray effectively before our creator as the scripture says . . . and now, in the later generations, as the tribulations are more frequent and sustenance is hard to come across . . . we thereby beseech our master, help us! Oh help us! You are our brothers, we are the sons of one man, aid us, aid us in prayer!

On October 18, 1830, Rabbi Israel signed his name to this extraordinary epistle. "The letter was given to Barukh ben Samuel of Pinsk, who was being dispatched to locate the Ten Tribes."[16] These faithful Jewish leaders, who longed for the priesthood and for the ordained leaders amongst the ten tribes to come and lead them to the Messiah, believed their mission had failed, when after four years of visiting every people he thought might have the keys he sought, Rabbi Barukh's mission ended with his murder in 1834.

Is it a coincidence that the Jerusalem rabbis were looking for a group of men who properly held the priesthood—at the very time that the Melchizedek priesthood was restored to Joseph Smith, the prophet? Joseph never knew of the letter from Rabbi Israel, but God was orchestrating His work and the restoration of His people. The Lord had promised "Behold, I, even I, will both search my sheep, and seek them out,"[17] and so, surely the eye of the Good Shepherd was upon Rabbi Israel and Rabbi Barukh and was reaching out to Joseph Smith, an Ephraimite,[18] even at the same time that He was instilling the desire within the rabbis to find their lost brethren, and the restoration of all the covenant blessings.

The gathering of Israel (including those who are adopted Israel) is the gathering of all who wish to join in the covenant promises and blessings given to Adam and Eve, Abraham and Sarah, and the faithful matriarchs and patriarchs through the ages.

Russell M. Nelson explained:

This doctrine of the gathering is one of the important teachings of The Church of Jesus Christ of Latter-day Saints. The Lord has declared: "I give unto you a sign . . . that I shall gather in, from their long dispersion, my people, O house of Israel, and shall establish again among them my Zion." The coming forth of the Book of Mormon is a sign to the entire world that the Lord has commenced to gather Israel and fulfill covenants He made to Abraham, Isaac, and Jacob. We not only teach this doctrine, but we participate in it. We do so as we help to gather the elect of the Lord on both sides of the veil.[19]

On another occasion, Russell M. Nelson said:

The gathering of Israel is the most important thing taking place on the earth today. Nothing else compares in magnitude, nothing else compares in importance, nothing else compares in majesty.[20]

The Lord promised:

And it shall come to pass that my people,

which are of the house of Israel,
shall be gathered home unto the lands of their possessions;
and my word also shall be gathered in one.
And I will show unto them that fight against my word
and against my people, who are of the house of Israel,
that I am God, and that I covenanted with Abraham
that I would remember his seed forever.[21]

While Jeremiah referred to the gathering, redemption and restoration of Israel as the greatest miracle, we know that that can only occur because the true "greatest miracle" ever performed is that which the Passover and The Day of Atonement foreshadowed: the Atonement of Jesus Christ, whereby all mankind can be delivered from the bondage of sin, redeemed, and taken to the Promised Land of the Celestial Kingdom. Today, we see Israel's borders enlarge, as all who take upon themselves the name of Christ are also called by the name of Israel, and Abraham.

These were the promises symbolized at the Feast of Tabernacles, as families turned to the sheltering protection of the *sukkah* to rest and rejoice in the shelter of the Lord.

---

1 Jeremiah 23:7–8, 30:3.

2 Jeremiah 16:14–16, 23:7–8.

3 Galatians 3:26–29.

4 2 Nephi 26:33.

5 Doctrine and Covenants 109:61–64.

6 1 Kings 8:41–43.

7 Smith, *History of the Church* 4:456–57.

8 2 Nephi 29:14.

9 Abraham 2:11.

10 Isaiah 49:22–23.

11 See Exodus 19:5–6.

12 Revelation 1:5–6.

13 Morgenstern, *Hastening Redemption: Messianism and the Resettlement of the Land of Israel*, 103.

14 Maimonides, *Sha'arei Zedeq le-Zera Yizhaq*, 40a.

15 Morgenstern, *Hastening Redemption: Messianism and the Resettlement of the Land of Israel*, 102.

16 Morgenstern, *Hastening Redemption: Messianism and the Resettlement of the Land of Israel*, 103.

17 Ezekiel 34:11.

18 *Journal of Discourses*, 2:268.

19 Nelson, "The Gathering of Scattered Israel," Oct. 2006 General Conference.

20 Nelson, "Hope of Israel," Worldwide Youth Devotional, June 3, 2018.

21 2 Nephi 29:14.

CHAPTER 35

——— ∽◦◦◦∾ ———

King Jesus and the
Hak'hel Ceremony

LeGrand Baker believed that the Savior's visit recorded in 3 Nephi closely follows the *Hak'hel* ceremony of the Feast of Tabernacles. Baker wrote:

> In third Nephi, this ceremony was not a dress rehearsal as it had been during the festival temple drama. The King was really Jehovah. He had come to *his* temple. The Holy of Holies was *his* throne room. In it was *his own* throne. No doubt the people who were present understood that what they were witnessing was the true enthronement—the reality for which the conclusion of the New Year's festival drama was only a preparatory enactment. When the Savior sat upon his throne, his feet would have been "established" upon a footstool containing their sacred emblems of his kingship and priesthood.[1]

Only the more righteous people remained in the New World after the devastating earthquakes and storms that swept the land at the death of Jesus.[2] The cataclysmic events, together with Jesus's invitation and teaching, seemed to echo that which had been foreshadowed in the fall feasts: 1) the call to awake and consider one's standing before God, 2) the urgent need to repent and prepare for the Day of Atonement, and one's judgment to life or death, 3) the gathering of the elect, 4) the invitation to come into the presence of God, represented by the *sukkah*, 5) followed by the specific invitation to eat in

God's company as symbolized in the Feast of Tabernacles, and the miraculous sacramental food that Jesus provided to the Nephites.

The call of the *shofar* had always signaled the beginning of the holy feast days. The *shofar* was known to represent the voice of God. Now, it was the very voice of God that called to the Nephites. Jesus did not speak in veiled symbolism, but directly and succinctly:

> *. . . will ye not now return unto me,*
> *and repent of your sins, and be converted,*
> *that I may heal you?*
> *Yea, verily I say unto you,*
> *if ye will come unto me ye shall have eternal life.*
> *Behold, mine arm of mercy is extended towards you,*
> *and whosoever will come, him will I receive;*
> *and blessed are those who come unto me.*[3]

One can't help but remember the teaching that instead of fearing to come to God after feeling the weight of the sacrifices associated with the Day of Atonement, one was to run to God and into His presence in the *sukkah*. Likewise, the Nephites who were filled with fear after witnessing the terrible devastation that fell upon the wicked, and experiencing the awful darkness that covered the earth, were invited to come into the arms of the Messiah.

As in the ancient *Hak'hel* ceremony, Jesus gave an account of His mission and His stewardship under God the Father,[4] recited the Law and covenant to the people,[5] and called upon them to repent[6] and to share the Gospel and gather others to it.[7]

Continuing in the pattern of Feast of Tabernacles ritual, Jesus promised the Nephite-Israelites that the Gospel would go forth to the Gentiles, and that the Gentiles would be gathered into Israel.[8] He also spoke of the unique relationship of the Gentiles to the House of Israel:

> *And I command you that ye shall write these sayings*
> *after I am gone,*
> *that if it so be that my people at Jerusalem,*
> *they who have seen me and been with me in my ministry,*
> *do not ask the Father in my name,*
> *that they may receive a knowledge of you by the Holy Ghost,*
> *and also of the other tribes whom they know not of,*

that these sayings which ye shall write
shall be kept and shall be manifested
unto the Gentiles,
that though the fulness of the Gentiles,
the remnant of their seed,
who shall be scattered forth upon the face of the earth
because of their unbelief,
may be brought in,
or may be brought to a knowledge of me, their Redeemer.[9]

The Lord invited all present to come and touch Him, and feel His wounds, that they might know for themselves that He is the Redeemer.[10] After doing so, they sang the Hosanna shout:

Hosanna! Blessed be the name of the Most High God! [11]

Again, later, He invited the people to bring their sick and afflicted unto Him, that He might heal them. The people bowed before Jesus, acknowledging Him as their Messiah, Savior, and King, and they "did worship Him."[12]

According to Baker, the traditional ceremony of the *Hak'hel* included the king providing a feast for his people at the end of his teachings.[13] Likewise, Jesus provided the feast of the sacrament for the Nephites (twice), and they were "filled."[14]

Still in keeping with the teachings of the Feast, Jesus promised the future gathering and harvest of Israel:

And I will remember the covenant
which I have made with my people;
and I have covenanted with them that I
would gather them together in mine own due time,
that I would give unto them again
the land of their fathers for their inheritance,
which is the land of Jerusalem,
which is the promised land unto them forever,
saith the Father.[15]

Part of the *sukkah* tradition is that the roof is to be "open" so that one can watch the heavens for signs of the coming Messiah. Jesus told the Nephites that He would give them a sign so that they might know when the promises of gathering and restoration were about to take place.[16] That gathering and restoration was an essential prelude to His Second Coming, when He would make a millennial home with His people. That sign was to be the coming forth of the record of the Nephites—The Book of Mormon. The Lord taught the Nephites that the Book would be given to the Gentiles, and come forth from the Gentiles to restore the covenants and gather Israel.[17]

Jesus spoke in depth about the close relationship of salvation between the Gentiles and the Israelites.[18] As we review His teachings, surely our hearts must be touched and moved with a desire to reach out to one another. There must be a healing and unity based upon understanding and compassion between the various peoples of the world. Only as we put aside our prejudices against one another can we come—together—unto Christ.

In conclusion, LeGrand Baker states:

> [The] similarity [to] the festival temple drama is unmistakable. The Savior had symbolically—yet literally—re-introduced the sons and daughters of Adam and Eve back into their paradisiacal Garden home where they could be in God's presence and eat freely of the fruit of the tree of life and drink from the river of the waters of life. . . . During his stay among the Nephites, their Savior-King had actualized the final events of the festival drama by instituting a new age—a time of peace and prosperity that endured for generations.
>
> As one considers the events of the Savior's coming to America, along with the concluding events of the Feast of Tabernacles temple drama, one realizes that the correlation between them is much too close to be a coincidence. The story itself bears witness that the author of the Book of Mormon was personally acquainted with ancient Israel's sacred temple rites and the ordinances that were necessary for eternal salvation.[19]

Let us be clear as to the "author" that Baker acknowledges. That author is *not* Joseph Smith, but various prophets in the ancient New World who recorded their testimonies as directed by Jehovah, Jesus Christ, that their record might go forth and be the prophesied tool of gathering and remembrance. The Book of Mormon is a companion to the Israelite Bible, and is another witness of Jesus Christ, with the express purpose to help prepare the world for His Second Coming.

---

1 Baker and Ricks, *Who Shall Ascend to the Hill of the Lord?*, 656.
2 3 Nephi 9:13, 10:12.
3 3 Nephi 9:13–14.
4 3 Nephi 9:15, 11:11, 35–36.
5 3 Nephi 9:20, 22, 11:21–28, 12:1–15:10.
6 3 Nephi 11:32–34, 37, 12:19, 27:20.
7 3 Nephi 11:41, 12:2, 15:22.
8 3 Nephi 16:13.
9 3 Nephi 16:4.
10 3 Nephi 11:14–15.
11 3 Nephi 11:17.
12 3 Nephi 11:12, 17, 17:10.
13 Baker, "The Savior's Coronation in Third Nephi," Neal A. Maxwell Institute Conference, 2008; Summary of *Who Shall Ascend to the Hill of the Lord?*
14 3 Nephi 18:1–9, 20:1–9.
15 3 Nephi 20:29.
16 3 Nephi 21:1–2.
17 3 Nephi 21:1–7, 3 Nephi 29:1–2.
18 See 3 Nephi 22:1–23:4.
19 Baker, "The Savior's Coronation in Third Nephi," Neal A. Maxwell Institute Conference, 2008; Summary of *Who Shall Ascend to the Hill of the Lord?*

CHAPTER 36

─── ⟨⟨⟩⟩ ───

The *Sukkah* Wedding *Chuppah* And the Marriage Supper of the Lord

And at midnight there was a cry made,
Behold, the bridegroom cometh; go ye out to meet him. . . .
the bridegroom came;
and they that were ready went in with him to the marriage.[1]

AS WE HAVE LEARNED, THE *SUKKAH* WAS A TEMPORARY DWELLING built especially for families to live in during the seven-day Feast of Tabernacles. The *sukkah* was to be built from leafy branches, representing a "living" structure, and the roof was meant to have numerous large openings through which a family could watch the heavens for the signs of the coming Messiah. The Feast is held during the fall, when nights are cooler, but still dry, and the full moon of the 15th of *Tishri* shines down from above, all contributing to the festive environment of the *sukkah*.

There is another celebratory structure that is of temporary design, like the *sukkah*. That is the traditional wedding *chuppah* under which a bride and groom are married. The *chuppah* originated in the 16th century, and is meant to represent the home of the bridegroom, to which he brings his bride.

In this context, the appearance of the bride and groom together under a *chuppah* before an assembly who have come to witness the event is in itself a public proclamation by them that they are now bonded together as man and wife. . . .

It is preferable for the *chuppah* to be outdoors, under the stars, symbolizing the hopes that the couple will be blessed with a large family, in conformity with God's blessing to Abraham: "I will greatly bless you, and I will exceedingly multiply your children as the stars in heaven." The *chuppah* in the open air is also reminiscent of the *sukkah*, a temporary structure erected during the holiday of *Sukkot*. Like the *sukkah*, the *chuppah* reminds the bride and groom that they are protected by God alone and that God is their only haven and support. . . . The *chuppah* literally means covering or safety and security.[2]

We have established the fact that many Jewish rabbis have long taught that the meeting of Israel with Jehovah at Sinai was a marriage betrothal, with the actual wedding yet to take place.[3] The covenant between the Lord and His people is viewed in this very intimate terminology. Israel Najara, a 16th-century poet and rabbi expressed this relationship beautifully in his writings. The following is included in Chapter 23 of this book, but now we read it in light of what we have learned of the seven feast days. Look for the symbols of the various feasts, and their teachings:

> *On the sixth day of the third month,*
> *the Invisible One came forth from Sinai.*
> *The bridegroom, ruler of rulers, prince of*
> *princes, said to his beloved (the people of Israel),*
> *who is beautiful as the moon, as radiant as the sun,*
> *as awesome as an army with great banners,*
> *Many days you will be mine and I will be your redeemer.*
> *I will honor, support, and maintain you.*
> *I will be your shelter and refuge in eternal mercy.*
> *I will give you the Torah by which you and your children*
> *will live in health and peace and harmony.*
> *May the Bridegroom rejoice with the Bride*
> *and the bride rejoice with the husband of her youth,*
> *while uttering words of praise . . .*
> *At dawn, on the fiftieth day since they had left Egypt,*
> *there was a long, loud blast of the ram's horn.*

The people came out of their tents
and saw that every part of Mount Sinai was smoking.
God had descended into the mountain.
Thunder crashed over their heads.
Lightning ripped through the air before their eyes.
The ram's horn grew louder and louder.
The people trembled. The mountain shook.
Moses said, "It is time to lead the bride to the bridegroom."
As Moses led the people to meet the Shechinah,
Mount Sinai in exaltation lifted off the earth
and hovered over the people like a wedding canopy. [4]

A *chuppah* or wedding canopy, as Najara refers to it, can also be used for a formal betrothal.[5] As the Israelites at Sinai were not yet ready for the fulness of a covenant relationship, that experience is understood to have been a betrothal, with a wedding to the Lord Jehovah yet to take place at His Second Coming, and the beginning of the Millennial Age.

Betrothals were as binding as marriages in ancient times. Ralph Gower explained:

> Once the arrangement to marry was entered into, there was a betrothal that was more binding than the engagement in contemporary society. The betrothal could be broken only by a legal transaction (in effect, a divorce), and the grounds for such termination was adultery.[6] Betrothal lasted for about twelve months, during which the home was to be prepared by the groom, and the wedding clothes would be prepared by the bride. The bride's family would prepare for the wedding festivities.[7]

With this emphasis on temporary shelters and homes as represented by the *sukkah* or the *chuppah*—and particularly, their connection to a home that is either built by God, or where one joins God in His home for a wedding or marriage—let us review Jesus's promise to prepare a home for His Bride. On the Passover evening prior to His death, Jesus reassured His apostles:

Let not your heart be troubled:
ye believe in God, believe also in me.
In my Father's house are many mansions:
if it were not so, I would have told you.
I go to prepare a place for you.
And if I go and prepare a place for you,
I will come again, and receive you unto myself;
that where I am, there ye may be also.[8]

Ancient Israelite wedding customs provide valuable insight into Jesus's promise to His disciples. In the period following a betrothal, the bridegroom would return to his father's home, or compound, to build a new home for himself and his new bride. The wedding could not take place until this new home was complete—and until it was approved by the bridegroom's father.

Zola Levitt explains:

We should appreciate that this was a complex undertaking for the bridegroom. He would actually build a separate building on his father's property, or decorate a room in his father's house. The bridal chamber had to be beautiful—one doesn't honeymoon just anywhere; and it had to be stocked with provisions since the bride and groom were going to remain inside for seven days. This construction project would ordinarily take the better part of a year.[9]

Donna B. Nielsen adds:

While the new home was under construction, the newly engaged couple did not see each other. If they needed to communicate, it was done by means of the 'friend of the bridegroom,' who carried messages between them during the betrothal period. The new home was built under the direct personal supervision of the groom's father . . . With such close identification between a father and his son, the father wanted everything regarding the bride's new home to be as beautiful and perfect as it could be. The quality of the workmanship portrayed the quality of the father's instructions and it was a visual representation of the groom's love and caring for his bride . . . The father of the groom was the sole judge of when the preparations were complete. When the father determined everything was ready, he gave permission for the son to claim his bride.[10]

Hopefully, an understanding of these wedding customs helps us to see the *sukkah* of the Feast of Tabernacles as something very precious and symbolic of the home that the Lord is preparing for us as individuals. *Now,* as we think of watching the heavens from the *sukkah,* we might feel great joy and anticipation in waiting for the Bridegroom to make His appearance. For, out of all the seasons, and all the feasts, none represents the wedding of Jehovah to His people more than does the Feast of Tabernacles.

> *For as the lightning cometh out of the east,*
> *and shineth even unto the west;*
> *so shall also the coming of the Son of man be.*
> *. . .And then shall appear the sign of the Son of man in heaven . . .*
> *But of that day and hour knoweth no man,*
> *no, not the angels of heaven, but my Father only.*[11]

Many people feel that the world has been waiting a long time for the Messiah to make His appearance, and some have given up hope. But, it would seem that it is the *Lord* who has been waiting for His *bride* to make herself ready for His coming. When John speaks of the "Marriage of the Lamb," he relates the timing of it to this statement: " . . . his wife hath made herself ready."[12]

Spencer W. Kimball wrote:

The time of Christ's return is affected by our conduct. . . . In my estimation, the Lord's timetable is directed a good deal by us. We speed up the clock or we slow the hands down, and we turn them back by our activities, and our procrastination.[13]

Are we ready and waiting in the sukkah *for the Lord to make His appearance? Are we watching the heavens—and the world—for the signs of His coming?*

> *Take ye heed, watch and pray: for ye know not when the time is.*
> *For the Son of Man is as a man taking a far journey,*
> *who left his house,*

and gave authority to his servants, and to every man his work,
and commanded the porter to watch.
Watch ye therefore: for ye know not when the master of the house
cometh, at even, or at midnight, or at the cockcrowing,
or in the morning:
Lest coming suddenly he find you sleeping.[14]

The Lord told the parable of the Ten Virgins to illustrate important principles so that we might be prepared for His coming, and for the ultimate marriage covenant relationship with Him.

Then shall the kingdom of heaven be likened unto ten virgins,
Which took their lamps, and went forth to meet the bridegroom.
And five of them were wise, and five were foolish.
They that were foolish took their lamps, and took no oil with them:
But the wise took oil in their vessels with their lamps.
While the bridegroom tarried, they all slumbered and slept.[15]

The time of the bridegroom's coming had been prolonged, and it was long past the hour when they had expected him. Their initial excitement had waned; they grew weary with waiting, and fell asleep in the deep slumber of forgetfulness.

Marvin J. Ashton explained:

It can be properly and appropriately concluded that the ten virgins represent the people of The Church of Jesus Christ, and not alone the rank and file of the world. The wise and foolish virgins, all of them, had been invited to the wedding supper; they had knowledge of the importance of the occasion. They were not pagans, heathens, or gentiles, nor were they known as corrupt or lost, but rather they were informed people who had the saving, exalting gospel in their possession, but had not made it the center of their lives. They knew the way, but were foolishly unprepared for the coming of the bridegroom. All, even the foolish ones, trimmed their lamps at his coming, but their oil was used up. In the most needed moment there was none available to refill their lamps. All had been warned their entire lives.

Today thousands of us are in a similar position. Through lack of patience and confidence, preparation has ceased. Others have lulled themselves to sleep to a complacency with the rationalization that midnight will never come.[16]

We know the rest of the parable: when the cry sounded at midnight that the bridegroom was on his way, all of the virgins looked to make sure their lights were burning, but five had their lamps go out while they slept. They brought no additional oil, and when they went to fetch more, they missed the opportunity to follow the procession to the bridegroom's home where the wedding feast took place. The door had been closed, and the virgins called out, "Lord, Lord, open to us. But he answered and said, Verily I say unto you, I know you not."[17] The Joseph Smith Translation adjusts this verse to the softer "Verily I say unto you, *ye know me not.*"

Donna B. Nielsen explains:

> When knocking at a door, an individual did not give his name, because it was felt than an impostor or thief might try to gain access by using the name of a family friend. His voice had to be recognized. This was a well-known custom anciently. There wasn't any spite on the part of the bridegroom or his father.[18] So, in the parable of the foolish virgins, when the Lord says "I know you not," he is saying that he does not recognize the virgins' voices. There hadn't been enough genuine interaction that their voices were familiar.[19]

When John describes the Marriage of the Lamb, and states that "his wife hath made herself ready,"[20] he links that readiness to dressing herself in "fine linen, clean and white."[21] Remember the ancient customs: at the time of the betrothal, a bridegroom would present his bride-to-be with fine fabrics from which she was to make her wedding garments. Clearly, the Lord is making a connection to the fact that His bride is to show her readiness to meet Him by what she is wearing . . . and if she has specifically made use of a gift of clothing He has provided for her.

What "bridal" clothing has been presented to the Lord's people? Anciently, fine, white linen was used for temple clothing by priests. *Are we dressed in the clothing that the Lord has provided as a sign that we are now ready to be one with Him? The wedding can not take place until we are.*

At midnight—well past the expected hour—the cry is heard: "Behold, the bridegroom cometh; go ye out to meet him!"[22]

According to custom, on the evening of the wedding, the bridegroom and "his friend" would begin a procession through the streets, knocking at doors, and asking, "Has anyone seen my bride?" The procession could take hours, and was full of gaiety as neighbors and friends brought their lamps and joined the procession. The bride waited in her parents' home where much care had been taken with her dressing; including braiding jewels and adornments in her hair.

Finally, when the groom and his procession of friends and neighbors arrived at the bride's house, the wedding could begin. We can visualize the story of the ten virgins within the context of this custom. But, we can also see how our Bridegroom, Jesus Christ, has had to "look through the streets" to see if His bride is prepared and waiting for Him. The book of Revelation suggests that she may have been deterred or distracted from her preparations.[23] The prophets of the Old Testament referred to the bride of the Lord as an adulterous wife, who went "whoring" after other gods.[24]

Let your loins be girded about, and your lights burning;
And ye yourselves like unto men that wait for their lord,
when he will return from the wedding;
that when he cometh and knocketh,
they may open unto him immediately.
Blessed are those servants,
whom the Lord when he cometh shall find watching: . . .
Be ye therefore ready also:
for the Son of man cometh at an hour when ye think not.[25]

Who then is a faithful and wise servant,
whom his lord hath made ruler over his household,
to give them meat in due season?
Blessed is that servant,
whom his lord when he cometh shall find so doing.[26]

The Lord asks us to do more than just watch and pray. He asks that we be *doing* His work, fulfilling the assignments He has given to us as His servants, and being a forerunner who prepares the way for His coming. We do that by sharing the good news of His Gospel with others as we tell the story of His love, of His Plan of Salvation, and of His desired reunion with each one of us. When we bring others to the Messiah, we bring them into the covenant of Israel, and we gather them home to God.

We have seen the use of the title *bride* as pertaining to Israel, pertaining to the Christian Church, and pertaining to the celestial city itself.[27] It is an all-inclusive title representing men and women from all races who will unite themselves in covenant with God. It is a covenant relationship so close that the Lord, Himself, refers to it as a marriage.

A bride took the name of her husband, even as we are each invited to take upon ourselves the name of Christ.[28] *How do we act in His name? What kinds of acts does His name give us* authority *to perform?*

Thou shalt not take the name of the Lord thy God in vain.[29]

As He spoke to His disciples on the Mount of Olives concerning His Second Coming, Jesus gave three parables to illustrate His concern about the readiness of His bride: The Parable of the Ten Virgins, The Parable of the Talents, and the Parable of the Sheep and Goats.[30] He had previously spoken other parables concerning these principles to a wider audience in the Parable of the Great Supper,[31] and the Parable of the Marriage of the King's Son, where He concluded "many are called, but few are chosen."[32]

We are all called to the covenant relationship with Christ—will we choose it?

It's interesting to see the link between the *lulav* that celebrants were to carry in their hands each day of the Feast of Tabernacles, and the coins of the Parable of the Talents, which Jesus spoke to illustrate the awareness and readiness of the bride. Think of how the Feast foreshadowed the wedding of the people to their God, as you consider that they were instructed to carry four kinds of "species" representing the living fruits of the land: willow, palm, myrtle, and citrus. The same "living" branches were used in the construction of the *sukkah*. God had gifted them with a land flowing with milk and honey, and they presented those fruits as a firstfruits offering back to Him, before they would partake of any of the harvest themselves.

In the Parable of the Talents, the Lord gifts individuals with "talents" or coins, that they either increased and improved upon, or buried. In ancient customs, a bridegroom would often present his prospective wife with coins that she would embroider into a headband and wear at the wedding. After the wedding, she would display the headband in a prominent location in her home, as a token of the marriage, but also as evidence of how much her husband valued her. The gifts presented to the bride—to each one of us—mark us as belonging to the Bridegroom.

Both the *lulav* and the talents represent the gifts of the Bridegroom, and both are carried, or held, in the hand. In both rituals, it is understood that that which has been given has come from God, and one must improve upon it, nurture it, grow it, and then return its increase to the Lord.

What has the Lord presented us with at the time of our "betrothal" to Him (this could be at baptism, temple endowment, etc.)? What have we done, and what are we doing with the gifts He has bestowed upon us? Have we arrayed ourselves, even as the bride, in His light, in His Atonement, and in the gifts He has given us, doing all that we can to improve upon them? Do we use those gifts in the service of others—His great sifting test to determine those who really belong to Him?[33]

A wedding feast was always a part of ancient wedding celebrations. We have seen how Jesus presented a sacramental feast to the Nephites, who were fully prepared to receive Him as King and enter into covenant with Him.[34] Today, the Lord invites us also to feast at His table of the sacrament. Using the same imagery, Nephi invites us to "feast upon the words of Christ,"[35] and Jacob urges us to "feast upon His love."[36] We look forward to the great "Marriage Supper of the Lamb" to be enjoyed when the Bridegroom returns, in which we will more fully comprehend what the Lord has prepared for us.[37]

Surely, the beautiful rituals of the fall feasts, and particularly, of the Feast of Tabernacles, with its familial celebrations in the *sukkah*, foreshadows the forthcoming return of the Messiah, and the great marriage celebration of the Lord to His people! May we learn from them, and ponder their symbols and teachings to help us to prepare our hearts and our lives to be ready to greet Him with joy—*running into the loving arms of His embrace.*

---

1 Matthew 25:6, 10.

2 "What is a Chuppah, and What Does it Symbolize?" *Vines of the Yarra Valley,* vinesoftheyarravalley.com.au.

3 See Chapter 23—Feast of Pentecost, Shavuot: The Betrothal of Jehovah to His People.

4 Wolkstein, *Treasures of the Heart: Holiday Stories that Reveal the Soul of Judaism,* 44, 51, 75–76.

5 "The Bridal Canopy (Chuppah)," chabad.org.

6 See Deuteronomy 22:24.

7 Gower, *New Manners and Customs of Bible Times,* 64–65.

8 John 14:1–3.

9 Levitt, *A Christian Love Story,* 3.

10 Nielsen, *Beloved Bridegroom,* 34–35.

11 Matthew 24:27, 30, 36.

12 Revelation 19:7.

13 Kimball, *Teachings of Spencer W. Kimball,* 441–42.

14 Mark 13:33–36.

15 Matthew 25:1–5.

16 Ashton, "A Time of Urgency," Apr. 1974 General Conference.

17 Matthew 25:10–12.

18 See Matthew 7:21–23.

19 Nielsen, *Beloved Bridegroom,* 50.

20 Revelation 19:7.

21 Revelation 19:8.

22 Matthew 25:6.

23 Revelation 19:7–8.

24 1 Chronicles 5:25; Jeremiah 3:8; Hosea 2.

25 Luke 12:35–37, 40.

26 Matthew 24:45–46.

27 Revelation 21:2.

28 Mosiah 5:8.

29 Exodus 20:7.

30 See Matthew 25.

31 Luke 14:16–24.

32 Matthew 22:1–14.

33 See Matthew 25:40, 45.

34 See Chapter 35—King Jesus and the Hak'hel Ceremony.

35 2 Nephi 32:3.

36 Jacob 3:2.

37 Revelation 19:7-9; Doctrine and Covenants 58:11, 65:1–4

— ❧❧ —

CHAPTER 37

Feast of Tabernacles, *Sukkot,* Work Chart

THERE ARE MANY SYMBOLS AND RITUALS ASSOCIATED WITH THE Feast of Tabernacles. Each of them can reveal something new and meaningful to you—and you will add additional meaning as you contemplate (or celebrate) the Feast year-by-year.

FEAST OF THE TABERNACLES

Symbol	Christ	Personal Insight/ Application
Sukkah		
Live in the *Sukkah* for Seven Days		

Symbol	Christ	Personal Insight/ Application
Lulav—The Four Species		
Water-pouring Ceremony		
Pool of Siloam		
Wine poured on the altar, same time as the water is poured		
The Giant Candelabra		
Huge willow branches arranged at the sides of the altar		
People shake their palms and sing Hosanna Shout		

Symbol	Christ	Personal Insight/ Application
The *Hak'hel* Ceremony— The king gives an accounting of his stewardship		
70 bullocks offered in sacrifice		
Gentiles must be adopted as Israel		
People to hear the Law (covenant) and accept or renew it		
Family meals to be eaten in the *Sukkah*		

Conclusion

JEHOVAH, WHO IS JESUS CHRIST, INSTITUTED AND GAVE INSTRUCtions concerning seven holy feast or festival days to be kept by all Israelites throughout their generations. Zechariah prophesied that the Feast of Tabernacles will be kept during the Millennium, and Ezekiel foresaw Passover celebrations during the same period.

The spring feasts—Passover, *Pesach*; Feast of Unleavened Bread, *Hag HaMatzot*; and Feast of Firstfruits, *Bikkurim*—foreshadow the first coming of the Messiah: His birth, life, Atonement, death, and resurrection.

The fall feasts—Feast of Trumpets, *Rosh Hashanah;* Day of Atonement, *Yom Kippur*; and Feast of Tabernacles, *Sukkot*—testify of His atoning sacrifice, but also foreshadow His Second Coming, and the Feast of the Bridegroom, or Marriage Supper of the Lamb.

The "middle" feast of Pentecost, *Shavuot*, celebrates the reception of the Law, or covenant, at Mt. Sinai, and the birth of Israel as a nation. It is also viewed as the betrothal of Jehovah to His people, Israel.

Israel is the name of God's covenant family, to which all people, regardless of heritage or bloodline, are invited to belong.

> *. . . and he inviteth them all to come unto him and partake of his goodness;*
> *and he denieth none that come unto him,*
> *black and white,*
> *bond and free,*
> *male and female;*
> *and he remembereth the heathen;*
> *and all are alike unto God.*[1]

Because the feasts and festivals were given by God to *all* Israelites, to be remembered throughout time, it may benefit us to become familiar with them, and to learn from their rituals and teachings. The choice to "keep" or celebrate the specific feast days is an individual decision, but whether one chooses to do so or not, the teachings surrounding them can enrich our own devotions and worship. We might set aside a week during Passover or Tabernacles, for example, to consider the powerful blessings that come through the Atonement of Jesus Christ, or to reflect upon our readiness for His Second Coming. Because the General Conferences of The Church of Jesus Christ of Latter-day Saints frequently occur during the same periods as the spring and fall feasts, members of the Church can incorporate a remembrance of the feasts in their own preparations surrounding Conference.

Because the fall feasts, in particular, look forward to the joining together of the Israelites and the Gentiles, both groups can enjoy a spirit of brotherhood, appreciation, love, and compassion during those festival seasons.

The more we know about the ancient feasts and festivals, the deeper our understanding and appreciation for the Messiah, Jesus Christ, grows. Through the feasts, we see many facets of His nature and character, from the submissive lamb taken to slaughter, to the triumphant and glorious Bridegroom come to take His people home to eternal glory.

> *And this is life eternal,*
> *that they might know thee*
> *the only true God,*
> *and Jesus Christ, whom thou hast sent.*[2]

---

1 2 Nephi 26:33.
2 John 17:3.

Bibliography

———— ❧ ————

Anderson, Karl Ricks. "The Kirtland Temple—'A Pentecost and a Time of Rejoicing.'" *Meridian Magazine*. Sept. 24, 2021.

Ashton, Marvin J. "A Time of Urgency." Apr. 1974 General Conference. www.churchofjesuschrist.org.

Baker, LeGrand. "The Savior's Coronation in Third Nephi." Neal A. Maxwell Institute Conference, 2008; "Summary" of *Who Shall Ascend to the Hill of the Lord?*.

Baker, LeGrand and Stephen David Ricks. *Who Shall Ascend Into the Hill of the Lord?: The Psalms in Israel's Temple Worship in the Old Testament and in the Book of Mormon*. United States: Eborn Books, 2009.

Boyd, Gale. *Days of Awe*. Independently Published, 2018.

"The Bridal Canopy (Chuppah)" and "Yachatz—Break the Middle Matzah." *Chabad-Lubavitch Media Center*. www.chabad.org.

Brown, Matthew B. *The Gate of Heaven: Insights on the Doctrines and Symbols of the Temple*. Salt Lake City: Covenant Communication, 1999.

Cherry, Lynda. *Redemption of the Bride: God's Redeeming Love for His Covenant People*. Utah: Cedar Fort, Inc., 2022.

Christofferson, D. Todd. "That They May Be One in Us." Oct. 2002 General Conference. www.churchofjesuschrist.org.

Chumney, Edward. *The Seven Festivals of the Messiah*. United States: Treasure House, 1994.

Edersheim, Alfred. *Sketches of a Jewish Social Life*. Massachusetts, US: Hendrickson Pub., 1994.

Edersheim, Alfred. *The Life and Times of Jesus the Messiah*. Massachusetts, US: Hendrickson Pub., 1993.

Edersheim, Alfred. *The Temple: Its Ministry and Services as They Were at the Time of Jesus Christ*. Creative Media Partners, LLC, 2018.

Edgley, Richard C. "'The Condescension of God.'" *Ensign*. Dec. 2001.

"Enrichment Section C: The Importance of Symbols." *Old Testament Student Manual Genesis–2 Samuel*, 113. Salt Lake City: The Church of Jesus Christ of Latter-day Saints, 2003.

Fisher, Sarah. "Moed: The Creator's Appointed Times." *Hebrew Word Lessons*. 16 Sept. 2018. hebrewwordlessons.com.

Gospel Principles. Salt Lake City: The Church of Jesus Christ of Latter-day Saints, 2011. www.churchofjesuschrist.org/study/manual/gospel-principles.

Gower, Ralph. *The New Manners and Customs of Bible Times*. United States: Moody Publishers, 2005.

The Guide to the Scriptures. Salt Lake City: The Church of Jesus Christ of Latter-day Saints, 2013. www.churchofjesuschrist.org/study/scriptures/gs.

Haymond, Bryce. "Who were the Shepherds in the Christmas Story?" *Temple Study: Sustaining and Defending the LDS Temple*. 18 Dec. 2009. www.templestudy.com.

Hinckley, Gordon B. "The Wondrous and True Story of Christmas." *Ensign.* Dec. 2000.

Holland, Jeffrey R. "'This Do in Remembrance of Me.'" Oct. 1995 General Conference. www.churchofjesuschrist.org.

"The Holy Temple: Rosh Hashana" and "Three Mitzvot." *Temple Institute.* 2020. templeinstitute.org.

Hunter, Howard W. "He Is Risen." Apr. 1988 General Conference. www.churchofjesuschrist.org.

"Introduction to Leviticus." *Old Testament Seminary Teacher Manual.* Salt Lake City: The Church of Jesus Christ of Latter-day Saints, 2015.

Josephus. *War 6.9.3.* Peabody, Massachusetts, US: Hendrickson Publishers Inc., 1987.

Jukes, Andrew. *The Law of the Offerings.* Germany: Jazzybee Verlag, 2018.

Kimball, Spencer W. *The Teachings of Spencer W. Kimball.* Edited by Edward L. Kimball. Salt Lake City: Bookcraft, 1982.

Levitt, Zola. *A Christian Love Story.* United States: Zola Levitt Ministries, Inc., 1978.

Lund, Gerald N. *Jesus Christ, Key to the Plan of Salvation.* Salt Lake City: Deseret Book, 1991.

Lund, Gerald N. "What the Atoning Sacrifice Meant for Jesus." *My Redeemer Lives!* Ed. Richard Neitzel Holzapfel and Kent P. Jackson. Provo, UT: Religious Studies Center, Brigham Young University, 2011.

Maimonides. *Sha'arei Zedeq le-Zera Yizhaq*, 14a, as quoted by Arie Morgenstern, *Hastening Redemption: Messianism and the Resettlement of the Land of Israel*, United States: Oxford University Press, 2006. 100–101.

Maines, Ronald D. "What exactly does it mean when we are 'set apart' for a Church calling?" Feb. 1992 *Ensign.*

Maxwell, Neal A. "Enduring Well." Apr. 1997 General Conference. www.churchofjesuschrist.org.

Maxwell, Neal A. *The Neal A. Maxwell Quote Book.* Edited by Cory H. Maxwell. Salt Lake City: Deseret Book, 2009.

Maxwell, Neal A. "'Overcome . . . Even As I Overcame.'" Apr. 1987 General Conference. www.churchofjesuschrist.org.

Maxwell, Neal A. "'Plow in Hope.'" Apr. 2001 General Conference. www.churchofjesuschrist.org.

Maxwell, Neal A. "Swallowed Up in the Will of the Father." Oct. 1995 General Conference. www.churchofjesuschrist.org.

McConkie, Bruce R. *Doctrinal New Testament Commentary.* 3 vols. Salt Lake City: Bookcraft, 1965–73.

McConkie, Bruce R. *The Mortal Messiah: From Bethlehem to Calvary.* Salt Lake City: Deseret Book, 1990.

McConkie, Bruce R. "The Purifying Power of Gethsemane." Apr. 1985 General Conference. www.churchofjesuschrist.org.

Monson, Thomas S. "Hands." Oct. 1972 General Conference. www.churchofjesuschrist.org.

Morgenstern, Arie. *Hastening Redemption: Messianism and the Resettlement of the Land of Israel,* United States: Oxford University Press, 2006.

Morris, George Q. In Conference Report, Apr. 1956. 112. archive.org/details/conferencereport.

"Mysteries of the Shofar." *House of David Ministries.* June 1, 2020. www.thehouseofdavid.org.

Nelson, Russell M. "Children of the Covenant." Apr. 1995 General Conference. www.churchofjesuschrist.org.

Nelson, Russell M. "The Creation." Apr. 2000 General Conference. www.churchofjesuschrist.org.

Nelson, Russell M. "The Gathering of Scattered Israel." Oct. 2006 General Conference. www.churchofjesuschrist.org.

Nelson, Russell M. and Wendy W. "Hope of Israel." Worldwide Youth Devotional. June 3, 2018. www.churchofjesuschrist.org.

Nielsen, Donna B. *Beloved Bridegroom: Finding Christ in Ancient Jewish Marriage and Family Customs.* United States: Onyx Press, 1999.

Pack, Heather R. and Daniel Smith. "Who Were the Shepherds." *Redeemer of Israel.* 20 Dec. 2020. www.redeemerofisrael.org.

Patai, Raphael. *Sex and Family in the Bible and the Middle East.* United States: Doubleday, 1959.

Pitre, Brant. *Jesus the Bridegroom: The Greatest Love Story Ever Told.* United States: Crown Publishing Group, 2018.

Pratt, John P. "Passover—Was It Symbolic of His Coming?" *Ensign.* Jan. 1994.

Prentice, Cynthia. "Leil Chimurim—The Night of Watching." 9 Apr. 2012. ourrabbijesus.com/the-night-of-watching/.

"Priesthood, Part 1: The Garments of the Priesthood." *Judeo-Christian Clarion.* https://judeo-christianclarion.com/teaching-letters/garments-of-priesthood/.

"Research and Perspectives: Recent Studies on the Book of Mormon." *Ensign.* June 1989.

Reuven, Yitzchak. Email message to author. Sept. 26, 2007.

Rich, Tracy R. "Days of Awe," "Halakhah: Jewish Law," and "Shavu'ot." *Judaism 101.* 2020. www.jewfaq.org.

Richman, Chaim. Email message to author. Sept. 12, 2007.

Ricks, Stephen D. "Kingship, Coronation, and Covenant in Mosiah 1–6." *King Benjamin's Speech: "That Ye May Learn Wisdom."* Provo, UT: Foundation for Ancient Research and Mormon Studies, 1998.

Schalk_and_Elsa. "A night of watching…a study of Exodus 12:42." *Set Apart People: Helping you be set apart unto Him.* 13 Mar. 2014. www.setapartpeople.com.

Schulweis, Harold. "The Hidden Matzah." *My Jewish Learning.* www.myjewishlearning.com.

Shana, Mikki. "A glimpse into the 'navel of the world.'" *The Jerusalem Post,* 17 May 2019. www.jpost.com.

Silverman, Morris. *High Holiday Prayer Book.* United States: Prayer Book Press, 1948.

Smith, Joseph Fielding, *Doctrines of Salvation,* comp. Bruce R. McConkie, 3 vols., Salt Lake City: Bookcraft, 1954–56, 2:340.

Smith, Joseph. *History of The Church of Jesus Christ of Latter-day Saints.* Edited by B. H. Roberts. 2d ed. rev., 7 vols. Salt Lake City: The Church of Jesus Christ of Latter-day Saints, 1932–51.

Smith, Joseph. *Teachings of the Prophet Joseph Smith.* Selected by Joseph Fielding Smith. Salt Lake City: Deseret Book, 1976.

Talmage, James E. *Jesus the Christ.* Salt Lake City: The Church of Jesus Christ of Latter-day Saints, 2006.

Treseder, Terry W. "Passover Promises Fulfilled in the Last Supper." *Ensign.* Apr. 1990.

Tvedtnes, John A. "King Benjamin and the Feast of Tabernacles." *Maxwell Institute, BYU.* 1990. publications.mi.byu.edu/ fullscreen/?pub=1129&index=8.

Uchtdorf, Dieter F. "'Lord, Is It I?'" Oct. 2014 General Conference. www.churchofjesuschrist.org.

Wersen, Bruce. "Keeping Watch: The Rabbinical Shepherds of Bethlehem." 23 Dec. 2012. www.hisplacechurch.com.

"What is a Chuppah, and What Does it Symbolise?" *Vines of the Yarra Valley.* 2020. vinesoftheyarravalley.com.au.

Wilson, William. *Wilson's Old Testament Word Studies.* United Kingdom: Hendrickson Publishers, 1990.

Wolkstein, Diane. *Treasures of the Heart: Holiday Stories that Reveal the Soul of Judaism.* United Kingdom: Schocken Books, 2003.

About the Author

———⸿———

By Marlena Tanya Muchnick-Baker, Author of
A Mormon's Guide to Judaism
B'Nai Shalom Gathering, March 29, 2018—Passover

LYNDA CHERRY HAS THE SOUL OF A JEW. SHE TAUGHT ME MORE about being Jewish than I learned in synagogue as a youth and as an adult. She has hutzpah. She knows her stuff.

Before I met Sister Cherry, I heard of her ability to absorb vast amounts of ancient and modern scripture, then like someone who has come to Earth for just that purpose, examine each bit, investigate and analyze it, weigh the concepts and the particulars according to their intrinsic worth, scope, color, and hue, then gather it all up, and, like an artist or an attorney before the bar, or like an architect exposing the whole Plan of Salvation before our limited sight, lovingly and happily delivers it perfectly and perfectly true.

Lynda lives **in** the Gospel. It houses her. She knows each room of it. She rests under the blanket of missionary zeal, she feasts at Heavenly Father's table. She loves all whom she teaches. Her audience is her joy. Those who attend her classes learn and learn and learn.

Lynda was born Gentile and Jew, the supreme ethnic combination for success. Her grasp of scripture is amazing and so is her memory. We love her. I love her.

———⸿———

LYNDA CHERRY IS THE AUTHOR OF THE BOOK, *The Redemption of the Bride: God's Redeeming Love for His Covenant People,* and the forthcoming book: *Judah and Joseph Reunited: The Hope for Israel.*

She is the host of the "Come Follow Me Made Easier" podcast presented by Cedar Fort Books.

As a convert of more than forty years, Lynda brings with her a rich heritage and understanding. With her background of evangelistic Christianity, combined with her love of the Jewish people, and her desire to bring all into the family of covenant Israel, Lynda brings a unique perspective to her work, seeking to build bridges of connection, unity and understanding between the different faith groups, as well as demonstrate the fulfillment of covenant promises through the Restoration.

Lynda has taught BYU Continuing Education, Institute, Seminary, and Adult Education classes, as well as Gospel Doctrine for more than 30 years. She has been a guest lecturer at BYU Education Week, B'Nai Shalom, and many firesides. She has led tour groups to the Holy Lands of Egypt, Jordan, and Israel. She has served as president of the Relief Society, Young Women, and Primary organizations of The Church of Jesus Christ of Latter-day Saints.